KU-514-321

60358

A Handbook for Teaching Sports

The National Coaching Foundation,
commissioned by VSO Books,
with acknowledgement to Anne Simpkin

Heinemann VSO

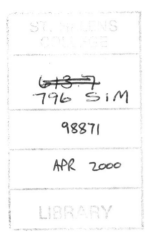

Heinemann Educational Publishers
A Division of Heinemann Publishers (Oxford) Ltd
Halley Court, Jordan Hill, Oxford OX2 8EJ

Heinemann: A Division of Reed Publishing (USA) Inc.
361 Hanover Street, Portsmouth, NH 03801-3912, USA

Heinemann Educational Books (Nigeria) Ltd
PMB 5205, Ibadan

Heinemann Educational Botswana Publishers (Pty) Ltd
PO Box 10103, Village Post Office, Gaborone, Botswana

FLORENCE PRAGUE MADRID ATHENS MELBOURNE AUCKLAND
SINGAPORE TOKYO CHICAGO PORTSMOUTH (NH) SAO PAULO
IBADAN GABORONE KAMPALA NAIROBI JOHANNESBURG MEXICO CITY

© Voluntary Service Overseas 1998
Voluntary Service Overseas
317 Putney Bridge Road
London SW15 2PN

First published by Heinemann Educational Publishers in 1998

British Library Cataloguing in Publication Data
A catalogue record for this book is available from the British Library.

Cover design by Threefold and Susan Clarke
Cover illustration by Shelagh McNicholas
Text design by Susan Clarke, Reading, Berkshire
Illustrations by Shelagh McNicholas and Susan Clarke

Printed and bound in Great Britain by Scotprint Ltd

ISBN 0 435 92320X

98 99 9 8 7 6 5 4 3 2 1

Acknowledgements
The National Coaching Foundation (NCF) would like to thank Penny Crisfield (review)
and Claire Vass (research).

VSO and NCF also wish to thank the following VSO volunteers, their colleagues and
others working in sports and physical education for the ideas, activities, comments and
materials they have contributed to this book:
Nic L'Anson, **Bhutan**; Ben Nartey and Rachel Tarr, **Ghana**; Peter Bryant, Marcy Chan,
Daryl and Sue Phillips, and Lolita Phang, **Guyana**; Joanna Glover, John Michuku
Marangu, Mr Muthoka, Mr Mwangangi and Juliet Perks, **Kenya**; Shinobu Hata, Simon
Lloyd, Justice Mahilasi and Grace Sithole, **Malawi**; Daniela Klockgether, R. Gonzalez
Gomez, Paul McLoughlin and Pauline Yemm, **Namibia**; Frankie Claxton, Declan Hamblin
and David Rake, **Nevis**; Eugene Clerkin, Camilla Marland and Jane Miller, **Pakistan**; Matt
Foulkes, **St Kitts**; Jo Neale, **Sierra Leone**; Joanna White, **South Africa**; Gareth Jones,
Tanzania; Bill Beattie and Bernard and Eva Batchelor, **Tonga**; Oluba Charles and Omara
Okeya Kaziro, **Uganda**; Musheke Kakuwa, Charles Lwanga, Oscar Mwaanga, F.M.
Nasilele, Simasiku Nyambe and Pam Rushton, **Zambia**; Simon Burrell, Samantha Darling,
Janet Moore, Mr Nyonyi, Elias Musangeya, Mr G. Segura and Angie Spicer, **Zimbabwe**.

The National Coaching Foundation provides a wide range of workshops and resources for
sports coaches and teachers at all levels. For further information and a list of resources,
please contact: The National Coaching Foundation, 114 Cardigan Road, Leeds LS6 3BJ, UK.
Web site: www.ncf.org.uk

Contents

VSO Books

VSO Books is the publishing unit of Voluntary Service Overseas. Since 1958 more than 22 000 skilled volunteers have worked alongside national colleagues in over 60 countries throughout the developing world. VSO Books draws on the wide range of professional experience of volunteers and their overseas partners to produce practical books and Working Papers in education and development. Care is taken to present each area of volunteer experience in the context of current thinking about development.

A wide readership will find VSO Books publications useful, ranging from development workers, project implementers and teachers, to project planners, policy-makers and ministry officials in the South.

Information from VSO Books can also be found on VSO's web site: www.oneworld.org/vso/

Other books in the VSO/ Heinemann Teachers' Guide series

The Maths Teachers' Handbook by Jane Portman and Jeremy Richardson, £5.25, 108pp, VSO/Heinemann, ISBN 0 435 923 18 8
This book is a vital resource for maths teachers in developing countries who are asked to deliver a mainly academic syllabus to large classes with few resources. This handbook contains practical activities and teaching tips for topics common to a range of syllabi, including guidance on the cultural context of mathematics and teaching pupils whose first language is not English.

How to Make and Use Visual Aids by Nicola Harford and Nicola Baird, £5.99, 128pp, VSO/Heinemann, ISBN 0 435 92317 X
This highly illustrated practical manual shows how to make a wide range of visual aids quickly and easily, using low cost materials which are simple to find or improvise anywhere in the world. Teachers, teacher trainers and development workers will find it indispensable.

The Science Teachers' Handbook by Andy Byers/Ann Childs/Chris Lainé, £4.50, 144pp, VSO/Heinemann, ISBN 0 435 92302 1
This handbook is full of exciting and practical ideas for demonstrating science in even the lowest-resourced classrooms. VSO teachers and their colleagues from around the world have developed these ideas to bring science to life using local resources and creativity.

Setting Up and Running a School Library by Nicola Baird, £4.99, 144pp, VSO/Heinemann, ISBN 0 435 92304 8
This lively and practical guide makes running a school library easy and fun. It has been written especially for non-librarians and because it is based on the work of VSO teachers and their colleagues working in low-resource situations, it takes into account the reality of schools in developing countries. Even with few resources it is possible to set up a school library that will make a real difference.

Books for development workers

Managing for a Change by Anthony Davies, £9.95, 164pp, VSO/ITP, ISBN 1 85339 399 1

Participatory Forestry – The process of change in India and Nepal by Mary Hobley, £14.95, 338pp, VSO/ODI, ISBN 0 85003 204 0

Care and Safe Use of Hospital Equipment by Muriel Skeet/David Fear, £5.00, 188pp, VSO Books, ISBN 0 9509050 5 4

Adult Literacy – A handbook for development workers by Paul Fordham/Deryn Holland/Juliet Millican, £8.95, 192pp, VSO/Oxfam Publications, ISBN 0 85598 315 9

Agriculture and Natural Resources Manual by Penelope Amerena, £9.95, 117pp, VSO, ISBN 0 9509050 3 8

Culture, Cash and Housing by Maurice Mitchell/Andy Bevan, £8.95, 128pp, VSO/ITP, ISBN 1 85339 153 0

Made in Africa – Learning from carpentry hand-tool projects by Janet Leek/Andrew Scott/Matthew Taylor, £5.95, 70pp, VSO/ITP, ISBN 1 85339 214 6

Water Supplies for Rural Communities by Colin and Mog Ball, £6.95, 56pp, VSO/ITP, ISBN 1 85339 112 3

Introductory Technology – A resource book by Adrian Owens, £9.95, 142pp, VSO/ITP, ISBN 1 85339 064 X

Using Technical Skills in Community Development by Jonathan Dawson, ed. Mog Ball, £5.95, 64pp, VSO/ITP, ISBN 1 853399 078 X

For more information about VSO Books, contact:
VSO Books
VSO
317 Putney Bridge Road
London SW15 2PN
UK
Tel: (+44) 0181 780 7200
Fax: (+44) 0181 780 7300
email: sbernau@vso.org.uk

Introduction

By the end of this chapter you should be able to explain why physical education and sport is of value to young people and the community, and understand how to use this book.

The importance of sport and physical education

Many people are interested in sports, particularly big events like the football World Cup, the Olympic Games, and the African Cup of Nations. In schools throughout the developing world, however, teachers face many constraints when they teach sports. Most schools do not have specially trained sports teachers or much equipment, for example many might only have one football. Students and other teachers might see sports as less important than academic subjects, and even if sport is a syllabus subject, teachers might not have training in how to teach it.

Sport and physical education can improve people's lives in many ways. Children in particular will benefit from the opportunities sport can offer. Their experiences will stay with them through their lives and may be passed on to future generations. Sport gives people the chance to:

▶ **get together and have fun** everyone can enjoy the social aspect of taking part in sport whatever their standard or ability

▶ **experience success and achievement** sport gives people the chance to improve their personal performances, fulfil their potential, participate in and win competitions

▶ **keep fit and healthy** sport can help physical conditioning, general fitness and well-being

▶ **learn physical and technical skills** students can learn about the techniques of various sports and how to improve their current skills

▶ **develop timing, balance and co-ordination** sport helps students develop these skills, which will be useful after leaving school

▶ **improve mental skills** sport and competition encourages people to develop problem-solving and decision-making skills, concentration, determination, control of emotions and commitment

▶ **co-operate and communicate with others** training and competing with others (particularly in team events) will encourage people to express and share their feelings with others

▶ **enhance motivation, organisation, leadership and interpersonal skills** sport can act as a way to develop these skills and take on responsibilities, which can be transferred to other aspects of life in the community.

How to use this book

Who is it for?

This sports and physical education handbook is a guide for primary and secondary school teachers, and anyone involved with teaching young people sport, for example youth and community workers and refugee camp workers, in developing countries. **You do not need to have experience of teaching sports or a lot of expensive equipment in order to use this book.** Many of you may have no training in sports, very limited resources and large numbers of students to teach at one time. This book will help you teach sport whatever your situation. It can either complement a physical education syllabus or serve as a complete guide for teaching sport.

How will it help?

The book shows you how to teach sports to your students. It explains how to develop skills and play games. There are many diagrams and pictures to help you understand these. The information is very practical and will help you to run sessions that are fun and educational. It covers many things you will need to know about when teaching sport, and explains why these are important. Many of you will have different needs and therefore you are encouraged to use the information to suit your own circumstances, for example in terms of resources, number of students, ages and starting levels. **Throughout the book we have used the experiences of and recommendations from VSO volunteers and their national colleagues, working in schools and with youth groups worldwide.**

What areas does it cover?

Basic skills are the foundation skills for all sports. Students learn these skills before they attempt more specific skills. For example, if students cannot catch a large round soft ball, they will certainly find it difficult to catch a rugby ball. Basic skills include:
▶ running and jumping
▶ throwing and catching
▶ hitting and kicking.

This book will help you teach your students how to enjoy and play a wide range of different sports. You might be surprised that the book is not divided into a different chapter for each sport. The best way to teach sports is through introducing games and skills that relate to certain sports and not by asking students to play a full game of a sport straight away. This is because students have more opportunity in mini games to practise their skills because there are generally less people involved in a smaller playing area. As a result they are far more likely to enjoy the games and improve their skills.

Once your students can master some basic sports skills, you can then go on to teach them skills that relate more specifically to different sports. You will notice that these are grouped together into invasive, net, batting and fielding, and athletic games. This is because there are many similarities between certain sports. For example, both hockey and football are invasive team games where one team tries to invade the other team's territory and score a goal. Similar skills and tactics, such as running, dodging, passing, shooting and defending, are used and it is important students begin to understand this as they learn about sport.

Many of the rules for the various sports include mini versions as well as the full game. These mini games are extremely valuable because they help students to progress towards playing the full game. They give students the opportunity to learn how to use their skills in a competitive situation, without all the pressures of the full game, such as covering a larger area, remembering more rules, having more choices of who to pass to and where. While these games are ideal for children who are learning skills, who are not yet strong enough, quick enough or skilful enough to cope with the full game, you should not be misled into thinking they are only for younger or smaller children: **everyone should be encouraged to start by playing mini games**.

The largest section of this book shows you how to teach your students many sports activities and games, to help them learn about sport and give them the opportunity to benefit from all that sport can offer. However, there are also other issues involved with teaching sport that you need to know. Planning sessions, creating opportunities for participation and competition, and the way you teach are all very important. As you may have very few resources available, suggestions and advice on how to make equipment is vital so that your students can enjoy many sports and have as much involvement as possible in the different activities. This book therefore covers the following areas:

► general teaching guidelines on planning, equipment, safety and taking the session (Chapters 1, 2, 3 and 4)
► how to teach the basic skills of sport (Chapter 5)
► how to teach the skills required to play many different sports, including rules for basketball, netball, handball, football, hockey, rugby, volleyball, cricket, rounders, softball, long jump, 100 metres and shot put (Chapters 6, 7, 8 and 9)
► other useful information on organising competitions, officiating and setting up clubs (Chapter 10).

How can it work for you?

Whatever the age or ability of the students you are teaching, this book provides suitable games for them to play. It will help your students progress their skills so that they can play and enjoy a simplified/full version of various sports. The progressions are referred to as stages. By the last stage of a skill, for example for goal-throwing games, Stage 5, 2 versus 2 (see pages 62–63), you should be able to introduce students to a simplified version of the relevant sports and also the full version, according to the progress and ages of the students. You will find that the descriptions for each of the games include details of playing areas, safety and equipment which take into account the constraints of available resources. There are also diagrams to help you visualise how to play the different games and to highlight major teaching points. The sample session plans show you examples of how to plan, structure and take sessions, using the activities shown. The 'Teaching points' boxes suggest key questions and model answers.

This book gives you the flexibility of having a comprehensive guide for one particular sport or all of 12 sports, depending on your situation. It groups activities and rules for each sport according to type (invasive, net, striking, fielding or athletic games) and there may be subgroups within these, for example athletic activities are split into track and field events. This will help you and your students to distinguish similarities and differences between the sports, and learn how skills and tactics from one sport may be transferred to another.

Please refer to the Glossary on pages 158–159 for definitions of the key terms used in this book. In particular, you should check the definitions of sport, students and teachers, to see how they are used in this book.

How to use this book

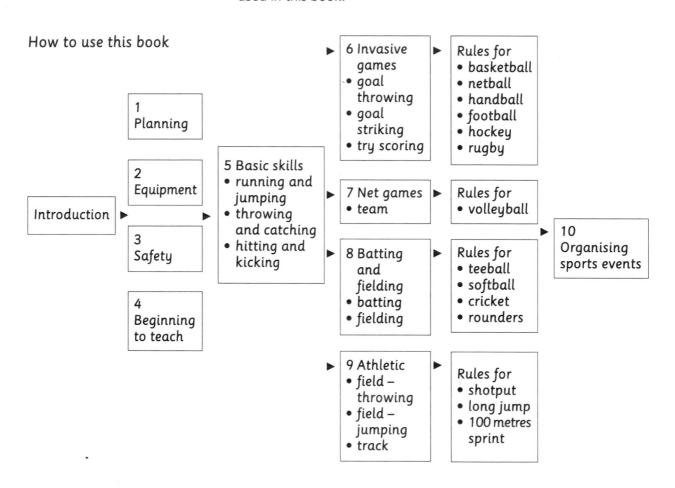

1
Planning a sports session

By the end of this chapter you should be able to:
▶ plan and organise sports sessions
▶ plan sessions that are safe, specific to the group and the individual, and that have clear objectives
▶ make or adapt equipment from local resources.

Why planning is important

Good sessions in sport do not just happen, they require good planning and organisation. Good planning can make all the difference to the safety, enjoyment and success of a session. Planning is particularly important when you teach large groups, groups with varied abilities and ages, and students with whom you are not familiar. It is also vital if your access to resources, equipment and space is limited. Time invested in thorough planning is time well spent. It helps you make the most of your teaching time and prevents time being wasted on irrelevant activities.

How to plan

The following session plans give you examples of how to plan a session. There is more to planning than writing a few ideas on a piece of paper. Students will be quick to notice if your sessions are poorly planned, and they will soon become bored. It is important you include variety in your sessions and split them into parts, for example warm-up 5 minutes, main content 20 minutes, cool-down 5 minutes. This helps you to plan time effectively and prevents important aspects of the session being missed due to lack of time. It is better to prepare too much rather than too little, providing you do not try to cram everything into one session. Activities you do not use in one session can be used in others. Consider the following factors when planning your sessions.
▶ Who will be in the sessions?
▶ What are the session goals?
▶ How will the sessions begin?
▶ What activities should be included?
▶ How can the sessions be kept safe?
▶ How will the sessions end?

Session plan

(FIRST SESSION)
<u>Date</u> 3.7.98
<u>Venue</u> Sunny School
<u>Time</u> 2 p.m.
<u>Duration</u> 45 minutes
<u>Group</u> Boys and girls, 8/9 years
<u>Number in group</u> 40

<u>Objectives</u>
To help students learn to throw and catch.

<u>Equipment</u>
▶ Targets, balls, bean bags, quoits, markers.

<u>Organisation</u>
Warm-up/introduction (5 minutes):
▶ three colours game (see page 24, warm-up activities for young children 1)
▶ drawing circles (see page 24, warm-up activities for young children 2)
▶ run to a mark, draw a circle (as above) with a ball, run back to base.

Main content (30 minutes – see page 44):
▶ 4 minutes – Activity 1, bounce and catch
▶ 4 minutes – Activity 2, up and catch
▶ 4 minutes – Activity 3, tap and bounce
▶ 4 minutes – Activity 4, high bounces
▶ 4 minutes – Activity 5, targets
▶ 4 minutes – Activity 6, quoits
▶ 6 minutes – relay game, race to a 15 m line and back while throwing and catching (as for Activities 1 and 2), pass the ball back to the next player in the team.

Teaching points

Ask the students

For throwing
▶ **How do you control your throw?**
Have a smooth action, watch the ball, follow through with your arm in the direction of the throw, keep your head steady.
▶ **How do you throw the ball to make it easier to catch?**
Throw the ball more slowly, closer to the receiving player and at a comfortable height.
▶ **How do you throw the ball to make it more difficult to catch?**
Throw the ball faster/harder, further from your body and higher/lower.

▶ **Which foot do you step forward with to throw the ball?**
Step forward with the opposite foot to your throwing arm.

For catching
▶ **How do you prepare to catch the ball?**
Move your feet into position, watch the ball as it approaches, keep your hands together.
▶ **How do you soften the impact of the ball?**
Relax your hands and arms, pull your hands in close to your chest as you catch the ball.

Cool down (5 minutes):
▶ walk twice around the playing area
▶ draw circles activity (see page 24, warm-up activities for young children 2).

Collect all equipment

Recap (5 minutes)
Summarise the main teaching points. Ask the students:
▶ How many balls did you catch out of 10 throws?
▶ Why did you drop the ball?
▶ Think of two things you have learned to help you improve your throwing and catching.

Safety
▶ Check there is enough playing area for both children and equipment.
▶ Injuries – none.

Evaluation
Students need more practice in all the games, particularly in Activities 5 and 6. Many students forget to follow through in the direction of the target and throw upwards and behind instead of

forward. Reinforce the need to follow through in the direction of the target and to keep the head steady.

Session plan

(SECOND SESSION)
Date 10.7.98
Venue Sunny School
Time 2 p.m.
Duration 45 minutes
Group Boys and girls, 8/9 years
Number in group 40

Objectives
To help students learn how to throw and catch in pairs.

Equipment
▶ Targets, balls, beanbags, quoits, markers.

Organisation
Warm-up/introduction (5 minutes):
▶ three colours game (see page 24, warm-up activities for young children 1)
▶ drawing circles game (see page 24, warm-up activities for young children 2)
▶ in pairs, roll the ball to your partner, your partner catches the ball, run to change places with your partner, and then repeat from the opposite position, your partner rolls the ball and you catch.

Main content (30 minutes):
▶ 10 minutes recap on Activities 1–6 as for Session 1; try to improve on scores from last week's session.

Games for two (see pages 45–46)
▶ 4 minutes – Activity 1, throw and catch
▶ 4 minutes – Activity 2, rugby catch
▶ 4 minutes – Activity 3, high and low
▶ 4 minutes – Activity 4, catch and run
▶ 4 minutes – relay game, play games 5 and 6 from session 1 as a relay; the first team to reach three points is the winner.

Teaching points

Ask the students

For throwing
▶ **How do you vary the height?**
Imagine throwing over or under something.
▶ **Where do you throw the ball if your partner is moving?**
Look for an indication from your partner; throw the ball in front of the body.

For catching
▶ **How can you prepare for the catch?**
Move your hands and feet into position, keep your head still.

Cool down (5 minutes):
▶ skip slowly for approximately 20 m, jog back, repeat
▶ stretch tall, crouch small, repeat.

Collect equipment

Recap (5 minutes)
Summarise the main teaching points. Ask the students:
▶ Did you find any improvement from last week?
▶ What was better?

► What did you still find difficult?
► What do you need to practise?

<u>Safety</u>
► Check there is enough playing area for both children and equipment.
► Injuries – Austen fell over, small graze on knee.

<u>Evaluation</u>
Students improved on activities from Session 1 but found new activities harder; they need more practice, particularly on game 4 (games for two).

Who will be in the sessions?

Before you plan the activities in your session, it is important to think about the students you are teaching. You can then prepare the sessions according to their needs and level of experience. The following examples show the sort of information you will need to know.

► How many students will be attending your session?
This helps you to visualise if there is enough space or equipment to carry out certain activities. Make sure you can adapt activities/sessions for more or fewer students, in case exact numbers do not arrive.

► What is the ability and experience of the students you are teaching?
For example are they complete beginners? Do they take part in any sport activities in or out of school? Are some students more experienced and skilful than others?

► What is the range in terms of physical and mental maturity of the group?
Sometimes age can be misleading as students develop at different rates, particularly in terms of size and strength levels.

► Are there boys and girls in the group?
Some activities may need to be adapted for mixed groups.

► What are the needs of the group?
Some groups may need more encouragement, guidance or time to practise than others.

Students with special needs can be involved in many of the games in this book, with some modifications. You should always include them in the main activity, unless there is a more appropriate game they can play. The students will tell you what they can or cannot do and you can then plan and adapt the session accordingly. You will have your own ideas on possible modifications to games or equipment.

Volunteers and colleagues suggest you encourage students in a wheelchair to use a cloth frisbee instead of a ball for throwing and catching: they should find this easier and more fun. The frisbee can be made by plaiting cloth and sewing it together at the edges.

What are the session objectives?

Planning helps you and your students to achieve objectives and ambitions. These objectives may be ones of enjoyment, participation or improving skill. Consider what the students want to gain from the sessions, as well as what you would like them to achieve, and then jot down the main objectives for each session. This has been done in the example session plans (see pages 9 and 11). Once you have clarified these, you can then plan the sessions so they include activities to help the students achieve group and personal targets. You are recommended to set objectives because it:

► helps you stay focused on what you and your group want to achieve
► gives you a basis on which to evaluate the session
► motivates you and your group to achieve targets
► helps you and your group to interact and creates a team effort
► provides opportunities for your students to experience success that will lead to greater enjoyment and self-confidence.

Setting objectives can hinder progress if they are not thought out carefully. For example, if you tell students they 'must' perform a certain skill by the end of the session, they may well react negatively to the pressure of this target. Listed below are some useful hints to help you set effective objectives for your session (with examples to show you how you would use these guidelines to improve the speed of your students). Try to ensure the objectives you set are 'SMARTER':

► **S**pecific For example for students to improve speed over 30 m.
► **M**easurable For example for students to decrease individual times by half a second.
► **A**greed with your students
► **R**ealistic For example explain to students that some will improve their time more than others; each student may aim to decrease their time by more or less than half a second.
► **T**ime-framed For example for students to reach their target by Session 4.
► **E**xciting For example explain how running faster will improve their sport.
► **R**ecorded Make a note of progress so students can see improvements.

How to begin the sessions

The start of each session is very important. It can affect students' attitudes towards learning, their enthusiasm, and their desire to have fun. It is often helpful to recap on the events and learning from the previous session. Ask the students what they remember! If they have been practising their skills since the previous session, you should acknowledge their efforts. In addition, you should try to:

► help groups relax

- explain the objectives of the session
- motivate groups to enjoy the activities and progress their skills
- prepare groups physically for exercise (see pages 23–26).

What activities should be included?

When you plan your sessions, consider the following factors.
- Are the activities varied but simple, challenging but achievable, fun but productive?
- Do they cater for the needs of the groups and individuals within the groups?

Planning the content of a session should be straightforward, once the objectives are established. The activities and exercises you choose should help those you teach to achieve their targets. Experiment with new ideas so you can add to your range of activities. This will help you provide variety for your groups and keep them motivated. For instance, when playing any sport you can always change the emphasis by making students play under certain conditions. In basketball, for example, if you want to encourage students to score goals using the backboard, you could make a condition that only goals having touched the backboard will count.

As a general rule, your sessions should include a combination of reinforcing what students already know or can do, new skills or challenges, and competitive opportunities. You should also note that students really appreciate and respond positively to a final exercise that is based upon fun and games rather than a technical skill.

When planning sessions for young children, you should:
- make sure your activities are suitable for their age, physical development and skill level
- change the form of the game to fit the children, for example modify the rules, equipment, court size, so that they can cope with the task
- make sure there are frequent breaks so that they can have a rest and a drink
- make sure you vary the exercises and keep each one short; young children get bored very easily and do not concentrate for very long on one activity
- teach them what they need and enjoy, as well as what you want them to learn.

How to keep sessions safe

In sport, accidents do sometimes happen, and teachers have a responsibility to try to stop them occurring. Sessions should start with a warm-up and finish with a cool-down to reduce the risk of

FOR ENCOURAGING EVERYONE TO TAKE PART

▶ Increase the options available, particularly for those who are not in teams, for example skill exercises or simple, fun games.

▶ Introduce new sports such as volleyball, basketball or softball.

▶ Introduce skills award schemes to motivate students by rewarding progress.

▶ Run competitions and present small prizes to winners and to those with other achievements, such as best effort, most improved player, fairest player.

▶ Encourage parents to support their children by coming to watch them in competitions.

▶ Give students leadership positions when working in groups.

▶ Give talks about sports heroes and personalities.

▶ Take students to watch a sporting event.

▶ Choose games that include fun, challenge and excitement.

▶ Recognise and praise achievement and effort during practices.

FOR ENCOURAGING GIRLS SPECIFICALLY TO TAKE PART

▶ Choose games that do not have an image of being gender specific, such as volleyball.

▶ Play with mixed teams of boys and girls, particularly in traditionally male-dominated sports such as football.

▶ Let them play and show you some of the games they are already familiar with.

▶ Let them take part in activities they enjoy, for example, keep-fit, rounders.

▶ Organise activities around the responsibilities many of the girls have in the home after school.

▶ Allow girls to wear clothes in which they feel comfortable.

▶ Promote sport to girls by using their pictures in publicity materials.

▶ Try to encourage community awareness of the benefits girls can experience from sport, for example, it can help to increase their confidence. This will help girls to feel that it is more socially and culturally acceptable for them to play sport.

FOR WORKING WITH LARGE NUMBERS

▶ Begin with a warm-up that is fun and will involve everybody.

▶ Divide the class into two with one group playing one game and the second group playing another.

▶ Ensure that each group includes some students who are more experienced and know the game well.

▶ Provide any students sitting out of the game with a ball so they can practise throwing and catching.

▶ Play rounders – this uses large groups and involves everyone.

▶ For demonstrations and warm-up exercises, stand with the group in a semi-circle around you. This means that everyone can see and hear you clearly and you can see them clearly too.

▶ Play winner stays on in games such as football or netball so when a team scores, the other team goes off and another comes on; this allows all students an opportunity to play.

▶ Play small games such as 4 versus 4 in netball using a smaller area such as a third of the netball court; this allows more games to take place.

▶ Divide the group into smaller groups and nominate a student to be the group leader.

FOR WORKING WITH DIFFERENT ABILITIES

Introduce new rules to your existing games to help students with less skill still enjoy competing with those who are more skilled. For example in games where the aim of the exercise is to score goals, you could introduce the following handicapping system: students with less skill score three points for each goal; those who are average score two points for each goal; and those who find scoring goals relatively easy, are only given one point for each goal.

STUDENTS WITH SPECIAL NEEDS

Working with students who have special needs is very rewarding, providing you understand their needs and feel confident of making the sessions work for them. Most important, you must make sure students with special needs feel integrated with everyone else in the session and are always included in decisions and activities, even though you may have to make some adaptations.* To do this, you need to find out more information. For example:

▶ What is the nature of their disability?

▶ What does this mean in terms of abilities and limitations?

▶ What does this mean in terms of communication?

▶ What are the needs of the student and how can you help to fulfil these?

* A useful book is 'Working with Disabled Sportspeople'. You can obtain it from Coachwise Ltd, 114 Cardigan Road, Headingley, Leeds LS6 4JQ, UK.

injury (see Chapter 3). The following list shows you examples of safety aspects that you should consider at all times throughout the planning phase. You should check:

- for obstacles or potential hazards, for example dangerous surfaces
- whether there is enough playing area for the number of children in the group
- that any equipment needed for the session is in safe working order
- the location of medical aids, for example first aid kit, water, the nearest medical adviser/official, clinic/health centre or first aider
- if any students have a specific medical condition, for example epilepsy, diabetes
- safe drinking water is available
- activities are managed, controlled and officiated properly
- students do not dehydrate: look out for signs of faintness.

One of the most common hazards in sport is people colliding with each other, particularly with large numbers and activities that involve running and chasing. You will find it helpful in many activities you teach to use grids. A grid is a playing area that is sectioned off by using four markers, one in each corner. You can give groups of students their own area in which to do activities but ensure that everyone stays within their own grid. This helps to use space efficiently and prevent students colliding with each other.

How to end the session

At the end of the session, always try to recap on what your groups have achieved. This reinforces progress and learning. Being positive at the end of your sessions will help to encourage students to practise some of their skills and look forward to the next session. You should ask your groups to help you clear away any equipment. Encourage them to drink plenty of water after the session as the body loses a lot of fluid during exercise. To prevent muscle soreness and injury, your groups should cool down (see page 26) at the end of each session and you should allow some time (approximately 5 minutes) for this when you plan your sessions.

After the session

One important stage often overlooked by teachers is evaluating a session or course of sessions. This is important because it forms the basis of future planning. It helps you to evaluate your progress as a teacher, as well as giving you feedback on the progress of your groups. Make notes as soon as possible after the session so that you have an accurate record. Your comments should include:

- what went well and why
- what went badly and why
- what improvements you can make to your sessions

- what changes you need to make to your next session, for example in terms of planning and equipment
- what the students enjoyed/disliked
- how the students behaved/responded/contributed
- how well the group achieved its objectives
- how individuals achieved their objectives; you should make a note of those who made good progress and those who need extra help.

You will notice a space for evaluation comments in the example plans on pages 9 to 12. Recording your thoughts on the plan will help you to remember the activities and goals of the session, and will be useful when you plan subsequent sessions.

Planning a series of sessions

To help your groups progress their skills, there needs to be continuity and progression from session to session. Taking a great one-off session is of little use if you never revisit the work covered; the chances are your groups will forget most of what they learned. Revisiting has many advantages because:
- it reinforces what students already know and stops them from forgetting
- it gives students a chance to evaluate themselves on their progress
- if there is improvement, confidence is boosted
- if there is no improvement, it lets students know they need more help and/or practice
- it gives you feedback on the effectiveness of your teaching
- it helps to clarify if students are ready to move on to the next stage or if they need more time on current activities
- students tend to appreciate a mixture of new challenges and going over familiar ground.

When you plan a course of sessions, for example over 6 weeks, you will have:
- individual session objectives, for example weekly
- mid-term objectives, for example after 3 weeks
- long-term objectives, for example after 6 weeks.

These objectives may have to be changed according to how quickly and effectively students learn. In order to keep objectives SMARTER, you need to revise them on a frequent basis. The session plans give you an example of how to progress from one session to the next.

Summary

Those who fail to plan, should prepare to fail.

Planning is an essential part of teaching sport. It is always better to prepare too much rather than too little; what is not needed immediately can always be used in another session. To help your groups progress their skills, it is vital that you think about what they are aiming to achieve. Once your goals are established, you can then plan your sessions accordingly and gather or make any necessary equipment. Regular evaluation will help you and those you teach to gain maximum satisfaction, fulfilment and enjoyment from the sessions.

2
Making equipment

By the end of this chapter you should be able to:
▶ make the most of existing resources
▶ know how to make or adapt materials to gather enough equipment for your sessions.

Why equipment is important

The equipment you use in your sessions can add to the variety and challenges you give to students, for example one ball can give your group the opportunity to practise endless skills and play various games. When planning sessions, it is important to answer the following questions.
▶ What equipment do you need to help you achieve the goals of the session?
▶ How many items do you need, for example how many balls or posts?
▶ Is any of the equipment you require readily available?

If the items you need are not at hand and need to be made or improvised, you will need to consider:
▶ how to gather materials, for example plastic bags, wood, string
▶ the cost of gathering necessary materials
▶ who will have the time and expertise to make the equipment
▶ how long the items will take to make.

The following guidelines show you how to make some items of equipment that are fundamental to many sports. They are all recommendations from VSO volunteers and colleagues. You may have ideas of your own to add to this list and the students themselves may also be able to help.

Remember that for many of the activities in this book, simple equipment will be all that is needed. For example, for throwing and catching games that do not involve the ball bouncing, items such as paper balls, rag balls, bean bags and cloth balls can all be used. Note that it is much better to gather lots of simple/improvised items that can be used in the games, than it is to use only one standard item, for example one netball, that has to be shared by the whole class. This is because one of the best ways to improve skills is to practise them repeatedly. With this in mind, you may find it necessary to give all your students tasks of making equipment in their first few sessions. This will help you to avoid being forced into starting the games without enough resources. Spending time on making equipment will always be time well spent.

The facilities you use may well be planned out. However, if all you have at present is a patch of land, you may find it useful to think of how you can make the best use of open space (see page 20).

How to make balls

To make balls from paper or plastic paper
▶ crush or roll up the paper or plastic paper into a basic ball shape
▶ use enough paper to form the required size
▶ use adhesive tape or rubber bands to hold the paper in place.

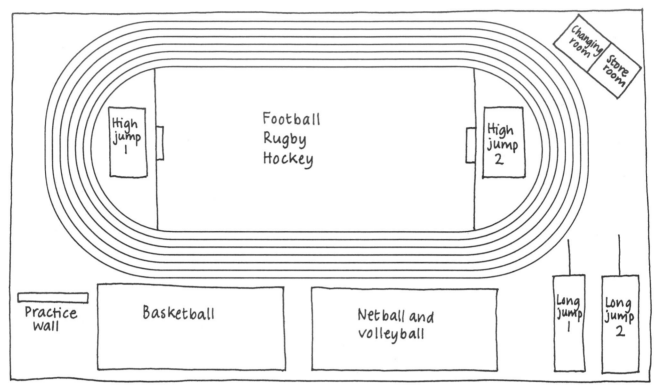

Note: Main field to be used for sports such as javelin, discus, shot putt and gymnastics

Volunteers and colleagues suggest that limited space could be used as shown above.

Volunteers and colleagues recommend that home-made balls are much better to use than cheap, imported balls. Imported balls are not designed to cope with rough ground and therefore can burst very quickly.

To make balls from socks or stockings

▶ fill a plastic bag with rice or sand until it is the required size of the ball
▶ fasten the bag with tape or a rubber band
▶ place the bag inside a sock or stocking
▶ twist the sock or stocking so it is tight and draw the top of the sock over the ball until there is no length of sock left.

Different sizes of balls are needed for different games.

▶ A ball measuring approximately 22 cm in circumference can be used for cricket, rounders, hockey, softball and the mini versions of these games. A heavy ball or stone of this size can be used for shot put.
▶ A ball measuring approximately 55 cm in circumference can be used for football, netball, handball, volleyball, basketball and the mini versions of these games.

How to make bats

To make wooden bats for cricket, rounders, softball and sticks for hockey

▶ cut tree branches to the required size
▶ for cricket and hockey, flatten one side of the bat
▶ for hockey, use sticks with a hook shape at one end.

Sand or water

Bottle

How to make markers

Markers can be made to use as posts for rounders, stumps for cricket, goalposts for handball, or corners for grids, by:
► filling an empty plastic bottle with water or sand
► or cutting sticks or branches to the required length and pushing them into the ground.

To make bases for softball and teeball, a take-off board for long jump or corners for grids
► use a flat piece of wood or painted tin can end which will show up well on the ground.

To make pitch markings
► use chalk, paint or pieces of string to define boundaries
► use a stick to score the ground and then fill the groove with ash.

How to make nets and posts

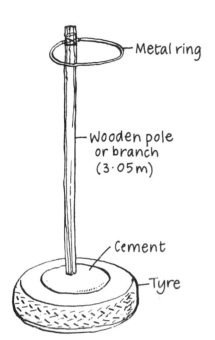

Metal ring

Wooden pole or branch (3·05 m)

Cement

Tyre

To make posts for netball or basketball from tree trunks or poles harvested from sisal plants:
► cut the branch or pole to the required length (approximately 3.05 m)
► dig the end into the ground for support or set the post with cement in a tyre for a base.

The ring can be made with metal and attached to the top of the pole.

For basketball and netball, a ring can be attached to a post in the same way or can be attached to a wall.

Posts for football, hockey, rugby, handball and rounders can be made by pushing wooden sticks or branches into the ground, or by cementing the ends in tyres for bases (as for netball posts).

To make nets for volleyball from wood and rope
► cut two wooden poles or branches to the required length (approximately 2.55 m)
► fix them into the ground, 9.5 m apart
► tie a piece of rope to the top of each post so it is pulled taut between the posts
► hang sisal fibres or strips of material from the rope (these make it easier to see whether the ball passes over or under the net)
► string or rope may be used to support the posts by attaching it to the top of the posts and to the ground with wooden stakes.

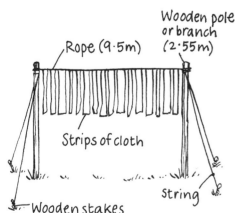

Rope (9·5 m)

Wooden pole or branch (2·55m)

Strips of cloth

Wooden stakes

String

How to make sports kit

For most sports, a minimum of clothing should be worn. Clothing should always be loose fitting to make movement easy.

A team kit can be easily improvised by wearing T-shirts of the same colour.

Bibs are markers that distinguish one team from another (for example by colour), and they can also be used to indicate positions. To make netball bibs:
- ▶ attach two squares of material (for the front and back) at the shoulders, leaving a hole for the head
- ▶ attach two strips of material on either side of the waist that can be tied together
- ▶ draw on letters for positions or sew on letters cut from material of a different colour.

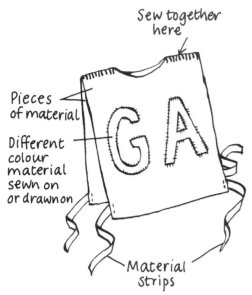

Sew together here

Pieces of material

Different colour material sewn on or drawn on

Material strips

How to make miscellaneous items

Many items in sport can be used to improvise equipment such as boundary lines, targets and goal areas. The following list suggests how to make these.
- ▶ Ropes can be made from sisal fibres, tree bark, animal skin (rubbed) or stripped tyre tubes (plaited).
- ▶ Bean bags can be made by sewing cloth together (10 cm x 10 cm) and filling with very small stones, beans, sawdust or any type of seed.
- ▶ Posts can be made out of bamboo canes or any straight sticks.
- ▶ Hoops can be made from wire, soft branches (which can be plaited) or hose pipes.
- ▶ Mats can be made from cardboard, reeds, sacks or empty 50 kg mealie-meal bags.

Summary

Equipment is vital to ensure your sessions run smoothly and students have sufficient opportunity to improve their skills. Remember that you do not always need standard equipment such as netballs or cricket balls; for many games you can use any type of ball. The more equipment you have, the more chance your students have to practise their skills, because it enables them to work in smaller groups and have more fun.

3

Preventing and dealing with injuries

By the end of this chapter, you should be able to identify ways of preventing injuries and know what to do if minor or more serious injuries occur.

Introduction

Accidents and minor injuries often occur during sport. Some sports by their nature are more dangerous than others, for example contact sports such as rugby. Teachers are responsible for taking every possible precaution to avoid accidents and injuries. However, sometimes they are unavoidable and you should therefore know what action to take if they do occur.

Keeping it safe

It is important for teachers in sport to create a safe setting for activities and games. Refer to pages 14 and 16 for safety aspects to consider when planning sessions. In addition, you should:
- always keep control of the group by demanding discipline from your students and ensuring they keep to the rules of the game or practice at all times
- teach your students safe practice so they do not have to rely on you
- ensure loose accessories, for example jewellery, are removed
- advise students to keep nails short and tie back long hair
- use a command or sound that tells the group when to stop or start an activity, for example the word 'stop'; make sure everyone can hear your instructions and respond quickly
- act if you foresee danger; it is better to be safe than sorry, even if sometimes accidents are narrowly missed and your concern is seen to be an overreaction
- adapt to the environment and the situation, for example avoid trying to teach rugby scrums when the game will be played on a hard surface; touch rugby is far safer.

Warm-up and cool-down

Warming up at the start of the session and cooling down at the end helps to prepare people for physical exercise, prevent injuries during exercise and avoid muscle stiffness afterwards.

Warm-up

During exercise, the body has to work hard to adapt to the increased demands being made upon its various systems. It is essential to prepare the body for these increased demands. Warming up makes the body less susceptible to injury and can also have a beneficial effect on performance, particularly at the start of a session or competition. You should include time (approximately 5 minutes) for the warm-up in your session plan (see pages 9 and 11) and include exercises that are relevant to the session. For young students, warm-up activities should be kept simple.

Examples of warm-up activities for young students

1 Start with some form of running game, starting at a slow pace and gradually increasing as the blood starts to circulate faster and the muscles and joints warm up.

For example, use three different coloured cards (such as red, yellow and green) to indicate an activity to be done. Show a yellow card and students jog slowly about the area; change to a red card and they stop and jump in the air; show both the red and yellow cards and they jog with a high bouncy knee lift or a long stride; show the green card and they run fast with small controlled steps into a space.

2 Then introduce a fun activity involving some gentle stretching and bending, for example of knees, ankles, arms, any parts that will be used later in the session.

Reach out to draw a circle slowly round the waist

For example, students might be encouraged to draw a big circle slowly round their waist by reaching out in front and drawing an imaginary line round to one side and then the other (with right hand and then the left); then crouch down and do the same thing on the floor; then, starting as high above (and behind) their head as possible, draw a big circle down to the floor and between their legs. Similar activities could be invented using a ball or passing an object from one child to another.

3 Finish with a more vigorous activity, where possible related to the activity to follow or revising skills or games used in the last session.

For example, if a football type game is to be played, try a three-person relay; each student dribbles the ball up and round a marker and passes back to the next player.

When teaching older or more experienced students, you may wish to follow more traditional warm-up guidelines.
▶ Gently exercise the whole body to raise the temperature, for example jogging, simple running games.
▶ Gently stretch the muscles (see opposite page).
▶ Introduce activities in the warm-up that relate to the session.
▶ Keep the time between warm-up and the following activity to a minimum.

Examples of basic stretches for most sport activities

Please note that stretches should always be done when the body is warm. They should be held for approximately 10 seconds and should not be forced to a point that is uncomfortable. Do not be tempted to bounce the stretch or stretch further than seems natural because this can cause injury. Repeat stretches at least twice.

Shoulder, forearms stretch
Link your fingers together, with your palms turned outwards. Extend your arms out in front at shoulder height until slight discomfort is felt in the shoulders and the middle of the upper back, arms, hands, fingers and wrist.

Back of upper arm, shoulder stretch
Hold the elbow of your right arm with your left hand and pull the elbow behind your head as shown, until slight discomfort is felt in the back of your upper arm and the top of the shoulders. Slowly return to the starting position and repeat with the left arm.

Side stretch
Stand with your feet shoulder width apart and your toes pointing forward. With your right arm extended above your head, bend sideways to the left from the hip (use the left hand as support) until slight discomfort is felt down the right side of the body. Slowly return to the starting point and repeat on the opposite side.

Quadriceps and ankle stretch
Stand facing the wall with your right leg bent and lifted behind. Support the bent leg with your hand and gently press the leg towards your right buttock. Repeat with the left leg.

Hamstring stretch
Lie on the floor with your back straight and raise your right leg as shown. Keep the left foot on the floor with your knee bent. Hold the right leg near to the ankle and gently pull it towards you until

slight discomfort is felt in the back of your thigh. Flex the foot of the raised leg to increase the stretch. Slowly return to the starting position and repeat with the left leg.

Calf stretch
Stand a short distance from the wall with your left leg in front of your right leg and support the body as shown. Keeping your back straight and your head up, move your hips forward until slight discomfort is felt in the right calf. Slowly return to the starting position and repeat with the left leg.

Hip flexor
Keeping your back straight, flex your right knee in front of your body (make sure your right knee is directly over your right foot) and

extend the left leg behind as shown. Move your hips forward and straight, keeping your buttocks pushed under; you should feel the stretch in your groin. Repeat with the opposite leg.

Groin stretch

Sit with the soles of your feet together, and rest your elbows against your knees as shown. Lean forward from the hips until you feel the stretch in the groin area. Keep your head up and do not be tempted to bend from the spine. Slowly return to the starting position.

Cool-down

To help students cool down in the most effective way, you should advise them to continue exercising gently for a short time (approximately 5–10 minutes) and not to stop immediately. This might include gentle jogging or walking and stretching. Cooling-down activities should never involve any vigorous movements.

Dealing with injuries

If you are taking a sports session, you are responsible for dealing with any injuries or illnesses that may occur; students will immediately turn to you for help. It is therefore important you know about:

▶ first aid
▶ emergency procedures
▶ minor injuries.

First aid

When you take sports sessions, you need to be familiar with basic first aid procedures. Make sure you know where to find the nearest first aider and, if possible, have a first aid kit at hand. Standard contents should cater for strapping and bandaging, cleansing and dressing. If you do not have access to a first aid kit, use clean water and clean material (preferably cotton) instead to clean any wounds. In the event of an injury, you should 'STOP':

▶ **S**top the activity and stay calm
▶ **T**alk to the injured student; reassure the student, ask what happened and whether or where he or she feels pain
▶ **O**bserve the student while speaking; is his or her behaviour normal or confused? Is any part of the body swollen? If you are worried, get help
▶ **P**revent further injury and decide if the injury is:
severe use your emergency action plan (see under Emergency procedures)

minor see under Minor injuries

very minor (for example a bruise or bump) advise the student to continue the activity carefully.

Emergency procedures

In case of emergencies, there must always be a plan of action. As each school is different, you must draw up your own plan. Make sure you:

▶ assess the situation and the injury
▶ know how to contact a first aider or other medical help
▶ know where you might get transport
▶ keep a note of the events, for example how the injury happened, when, what you saw and heard, for your own records and so you can pass on accurate information
▶ contact friends and family if necessary, and tell them the situation clearly and calmly.

Minor injuries

Most injuries in sport do not require emergency treatment. They need time and a sensible course of action to make a full recovery. It is important for injuries to be dealt with immediately to prevent further damage and to speed up the healing process. Here are some guidelines.

Cuts and grazes

Wash your hands, then wash the wound with running water if available and cover with a suitable dressing.

Bruises

Cool with ice or cold water, raise and support in a comfortable position.

Muscles, ligaments and tendons

Cool with ice or cold water, rest and support the injury. Wrap the injured part (with a bandage or some cloth) tightly and raise. This will help to reduce any swelling.

Please note Do not use heat or massage with any of the above injuries.

For minor injuries, remember 'RICE':

▶ **R**est Stop the activity immediately
▶ **I**ce Apply ice or cold water (see bruises above) to the injured area; you can protect skin from ice burns with a thin layer of cloth
▶ **C**ompress Wrap the injured area tightly with a bandage or some cloth
▶ **E**levate Raise the injured limb.

You should also help to prevent your students suffering from dehydration or heat exhaustion/exposure by encouraging them to:

Volunteers and colleagues suggest the following alternative if ice is not available: keep a plastic container filled with cold water and wrap it in a thick, wet cloth; as the water on the cloth evaporates, it cools the water in the container.

Volunteers and colleagues recommend the following procedures for some common injuries in sport. When dealing with:
▶ neck or back injuries: roll up newspaper to make a collar – this will reduce spinal movement
▶ broken bones: make a splint from sticks or wood and cover with rags – this will immobilise the limb
▶ sprained fingers: strap the injured finger with a bandage or piece of cloth to the next finger – this allows some movement but gives it support
▶ heat problems, cleaning cuts and reducing swelling: use cold water immediately and bandage if necessary – note that you should always have a bucket of water and some boiled or sterilised cloths nearby.

▶ drink plenty before, during and after exercise
▶ eat sensibly
▶ wear cool, breathable clothing, for example cotton T-shirts
▶ wear light-coloured clothing because dark colours retain more heat
▶ keep the sun off their heads and faces by wearing caps or similar items
▶ stay in the shade as much as possible.

It is important to remember that children cannot readily control their body temperature and tend to heat up and cool down more quickly than adults.

General guidelines for safe practice

As the person in charge of the session, you are advised to monitor the day-to-day health of those in your group. If students show signs of illness or injury, for example shivering or muscle soreness, during the session, you must decide whether they should continue. Most ailments become even worse under the strain of physical activity and therefore the safest option is always to stop.

Some injuries are accidental and unavoidable; others result from negligence or overuse when the body is tired. If students are tired or stressed, you may be wise to advise them to rest. If they do have an injury, be sure it has fully recovered before they return to sporting activities and build up the intensity gradually.

Remember that children:
▶ will experience growth spurts that may affect their strength and co-ordination; you may need to advise them to cut down on their activities while they are going through this phase
▶ cannot tell as easily as adults when they are tired and need to rest, eat or drink, keep warm or cool down; make sure you advise them as appropriate.

Encourage your students to adopt good habits. It is part of their education to learn how to play safely and look after themselves. For example encourage them to:
▶ play fairly and stick to the rules; rules are for safety as well as fair play
▶ listen carefully to your commands and never talk at the same time
▶ react quickly and sensibly to your commands at all times
▶ ask you if they do not understand something
▶ drink plenty of fluids before, during and after exercise
▶ replenish their food stores by eating after exercise
▶ avoid indigestion by not eating immediately prior to exercise
▶ make sure they have enough rest between sessions
▶ know when their bodies are weary and stop if they are very tired (especially children).

Summary

Teachers have an important responsibility for safety in sport. It should be a major consideration in session plans and you should know how to reduce the risk of injury and illness as well as how to deal with accidents, if they occur.

4
Beginning to teach sport

By the end of this chapter you should be able to make sessions productive, fun and motivating.

What is your role?

It is important to get to know the students you teach. Each will be different in some way. Once you understand them, you will be able to encourage them and help them all to make the most of their abilities. The more you get to know about sport and how to help others improve their skills, the more you will progress with your groups. However, sport is not just about teaching complicated skills. Your role includes acting as:

▶ **guardian** to ensure sessions are fun, safe and fair
▶ **organiser** to ensure every student gets the maximum opportunity and time in each session
▶ **motivator** to generate a positive and enthusiastic approach in each student
▶ **instructor** to help students acquire skills in a competitive and non-competitive environment
▶ **trainer** to improve physical fitness and health.

Motivation

One of your major roles as a sports teacher is motivating your groups. Not all students will be enthusiastic about taking part in sport, particularly if they fear they will not be very good. Your efforts will help students to fulfil their potential, and also help maintain the enthusiasm that they may already have. The following list gives you some tips on how to keep students motivated:

▶ keep the sessions fun
▶ be enthusiastic at all times; this has a positive effect on others
▶ keep students actively involved
▶ avoid long queues, students will soon lose interest
▶ help students to recognise what skills are needed and when
▶ help students to build on their own experiences and skills
▶ acknowledge improvements
▶ encourage effort rather than ability or winning
▶ keep information short and simple, particularly for younger students
▶ group students by ability; this may depend on their size and physical strength
▶ change the activities frequently to prevent boredom
▶ structure the session so everyone can feel a sense of achievement
▶ be sensitive to any pressures/anxieties students might have
▶ react positively to mistakes and encourage your groups to do the same
▶ do not allow students to pick teams; this can be very demoralising for those who are not so good.

Volunteers and colleagues suggest that asking a national sports personality to talk about fair play is an excellent way of helping students to appreciate its value.

Volunteers and colleagues suggest that awards for fair play motivate students to practise playing fairly. For example, you could award a prize to the team who appears to have enjoyed themselves the most or who have displayed the best sporting behaviour.

They also suggest, for example, that for netball, when students obstruct through bodily contact, they must stand with their feet apart for 2 minutes before they are allowed to continue. A further example is where students are banned from the game or activity for 5 minutes for unfair play. These forfeits can add to the excitement of an activity, as well as encouraging students not to make the same mistake again.

Volunteers and colleagues suggest that awarding prize money should always be avoided.

Encouraging fair play

In sport, many people are motivated by their desire to win. This can be positive, providing they also show respect, for example towards opponents and officials, and behave in a sporting manner. Encourage your students to appreciate the importance of fair play. Let them know that simply taking part in a fair game has many rewards. For example, those who play fairly will be respected not just as good sportspeople but as fair people in general. Your influence as the teacher, or person in charge of the session, will have a noticeable effect on how well students begin to understand the importance of fair play and put it into practice. You should therefore try to:

▶ set and maintain standards of fair play at all times
▶ lead by example
▶ emphasize the importance of participation
▶ be consistent in your approach and treat all students equally
▶ praise sporting behaviour as well as effort and performance
▶ teach students to play by the rules, accept decisions and, if they are not playing fairly, always explain to them why their behaviour is unacceptable
▶ penalise unfair play

Taking the session

Chapter 1 explains the importance of planning sessions and how to do this. However, there are other guidelines you can follow to help your sessions run smoothly on the day.

▶ Arrive in good time so you can check the safety of the playing area, go through the session plan, mark out grids and set out the equipment ready for when the students arrive.
▶ Explain the objectives of the session to the students.
▶ Make sure you know what you are going to say before you stop the group. Only call the students if you have something valuable to say. Check they can all see and hear you.
▶ When working with large groups, try to split them up into small subgroups. This helps the students to have more practice at the various activities.
▶ Always finish on time. Call the students together at the end of the session to recap, give feedback and suggest skills and activities they can practise on their own.
▶ Ask the group to help you collect any equipment you have used during the session; check that everything has been collected.

How to help students learn

If you are enthusiastic, you will encourage others to learn. The more enthusiastic you are, the more positively your students are likely to respond. Students learn best when they are:

- **actively involved in their own learning** when they are actually having a go
- **able to recognise how, why and when skills are used** when they learn how to apply the skills to a game
- **able to build on their own experience and skills** when practices are introduced progressively and linked to previous learning whenever possible
- **interested and motivated** when the sessions are fun and enjoyable
- **able to see their own improvements** when they recognise and feel positive differences
- **rewarded for effort as much as ability** for example when they are given praise for trying, even if they are unsuccessful
- **faced with a realistic chance of achieving success** when practices or games are neither too difficult nor too easy.

Stages of learning

Learning skills takes time. It requires going through a learning process. Understanding the various stages of the process will help you assess how quickly your students are developing skills. You can then give them feedback and adjust practices to suit different stages and rates of learning.

In the first stage, students need to understand what is required. Explain to them the aim of the practice or skill and make sure they have a clear picture in their mind of what they are trying to achieve. Keep practices short and simple and emphasise the nature of the task rather than the outcome, for example what the throw looks like as opposed to where or how far it goes.

By the second stage, students have grasped the basic idea of the task and need to improve the way they carry it out. The size and number of errors should start to reduce. Students should begin to make corrections automatically and you should, therefore, encourage them to use their own senses, for example sight, sound and touch, to obtain feedback about their actions.

At the third stage, students have no need to analyse the skill consciously or talk themselves through it. They have become experts and can carry out the skill effectively and automatically. They are usually able to detect their own errors and make appropriate corrections. However, there is still a need to maintain and refine the skill. Encourage students to practise and intervene only with very specific comments about the skill.

How to communicate

Effective communication is vital in teaching sport. It involves giving information *and* receiving it; talking *and* listening. You need to send the correct messages to your groups, but also to give them a chance to tell you how they are doing. Here are some guidelines.
- It is important to ask questions and listen carefully to answers.

- Make sure you have the attention of your group before you speak.
- Try to gain and maintain eye contact.
- Speak loud enough for everyone to hear but try not to shout.
- Remember actions speak louder than words – act positively at all times.
- Use simple words and do not give people too much information at any one time.
- Consider the age, experience and skill level of the students you are teaching and adapt your words and manner accordingly.
- Young students will feel more at ease if you kneel down to their level when you are talking with them. They may be more receptive if you let them sit down while you are talking.
- Encourage those you teach to ask if they do not understand.
- Use one clear word, for example 'stop', to attract attention.
- Use a short command, for example 'come round', once you have everyone's attention.
- Make sure your groups know when to begin an activity after you have called them round, for example 'off you go'.

Demonstration

Actions speak louder than words.

Most people find it easier to take in visual information rather than a long explanation. This means that demonstration is an extremely powerful teaching tool, although you must use it appropriately.
- Position the group so everyone can see the demonstration clearly and hear what you have to say, for example make sure no-one is behind you or looking directly into the sun.
- Make sure the demonstration is simple enough for the group to copy.
- Do not be tempted to tell the group everything at once; select one or two key points, for example 'watch my feet'.
- Repeat the demonstration at least twice.
- Let people have a go and give them sufficient time to practise.
- Use students in the group (rather than yourself) to demonstrate whenever possible.
- Encourage students to observe others and learn from their actions.

How to give positive feedback

Students like to know how they are doing and will often look to you for feedback. Your comments will inspire them but you should also encourage them to use information from their senses, for example 'Does the action feel right? What does it sound like? Where do you feel tension in the muscles?' Feedback helps the learning process as it can reinforce good practice and highlight how to improve further. Make sure your comments are positive.

Too often people are inclined to focus only on what is wrong, which can be very demoralising. Here are some tips for giving students positive feedback:

▶ build on what is good and show them how they can improve further

▶ encourage them to have a go; help them to believe they can do it

▶ make sure feedback is accurate and frequent; this helps the learning process and reduces the likelihood of reinforcing bad practice

▶ give feedback when it is needed and when it seems appropriate within the session; please note, it is possible to overdo feedback, which can cause students to lack confidence

▶ give credit only when credit is due but always acknowledge effort

▶ encourage students to give themselves feedback and not always to rely on others.

How to find out more on coaching sport

As your involvement in teaching sport increases, you will become more and more experienced. You will learn from observing and analysing the progress of those you teach, as well as learning from your own successes and mistakes (for example, why did that group progress faster than the other one?). If you want to learn more about teaching sport, the following introductory study packs are recommended. They are all published by the National Coaching Foundation and are available from Coachwise Ltd, 114 Cardigan Road, Headingley, Leeds LS6 4JQ, UK; telephone (+44)113 2311310, fax (+44)113 275 5019.

▶ *The coach in action*
▶ *The body in action*
▶ *Safety and injury*
▶ *Improving techniques*
▶ *Mind over matter*
▶ *Planning and practice*
▶ *Working with children*
▶ *Working with disabled sportspeople*

If you would like to read about teaching and coaching sport in further detail, *The successful coach* handbook is also recommended, from the same address.

If you are interested in setting up a sports club, the following booklets are recommended and are also available from Coachwise Ltd at the same address.

▶ *Running sport – running a club*
▶ *Running sport – starting a junior section.*

In addition, the *Sports leaders manual*, produced by the National

Sports Council of South Africa, is strongly recommended. The pack is in home-study format and covers many issues for those involved with teaching sports, including organising activities, competitions and clubs. It is available from: National Sports Council of South Africa, Johannesburg Stadium, 124 Van Beck Street, New Doornfontein 2094, PO 15510, South Africa; telephone (+27)11 402 1710, fax (+27)11 402 1724.

Summary

Teaching sport can be extremely rewarding. Your efforts can offer students much in terms of enjoyment, personal development and physical well-being. However, the way you teach and deliver sessions will determine how much they really gain from their involvement in sport. It is important you understand the learning process which takes place in skill development, and remember that effective communication, demonstration and feedback are important aspects of good sessions. Always strive to keep your group motivated and encourage fair play.

5
Introducing the basic skills of sport

By the end of this chapter you should be able to teach three basic skills of sport.

Introduction

When you introduce students to sport, it is important to start with some basic skills. Do not be tempted to think these skills are only necessary for children: they are vital for anyone of any age who is new to sport. As you become more familiar with teaching sport, you will notice that many sports are a combination of basic skills. Combining these skills can be complex and if you force students to try games that are too difficult for them, they will soon lose confidence and enthusiasm. Therefore, you should always encourage them to learn the basic skills before they attempt to play various sports. It is very important that you help them experience success in their first few sessions in particular, so that their image of sport is positive. Basic skills provide students with the foundation for learning more traditional games. They will find the activities in this chapter challenging but at a level they can enjoy. Basic skills can be grouped into the following categories:

▶ running and jumping, which includes dodging, chasing, hopping and skipping
▶ throwing and catching, which includes bouncing a ball
▶ hitting and kicking (a ball).

This chapter explains how these skills relate to different sports, for example throwing and catching skills will help students when they are introduced to sports such as netball and rugby. It shows you how to build on basic activities and we encourage you to add your own ideas to the examples given. In each group of skills there are a number of stages. The final stage indicates the point at which students should be ready to move on to more advanced skills, which will prepare them for specific sports (Chapters 6, 7, 8 and 9).

Running and jumping skills

Running and jumping skills provide essential grounding for track and field athletic events, for example sprints, hurdles, long jump and high jump (see Chapter 9). However, many sports require these types of athletic skills, for example jumping up for a catch, marking players, finding free space, reaching the ball before it bounces twice. These skills are also very effective in developing a base of fitness. They can improve endurance, strength and speed, and develop general co-ordination and movement of the body.

Stage 1 *Shuttle race*

Objectives
To teach students how to run and change direction quickly.

Equipment

▶ Three markers per team, for example plastic bottles or pieces of cloth.
▶ Markers to indicate starting line and lines 1 (10 m), 2 (20 m) and 3 (30 m). These markers should be different and larger than the markers each team has, for example a plastic bottle or a bundle. The lines can be indicated by drawing a line in the ground instead of using markers.

Safety

▶ Students should stay well behind the start line when it is not their turn.
▶ Teams should keep their distance from each other.
▶ Students should stay away from the markers.
▶ Students should look where they are running.

Activity

▶ In teams of four or six, each team must have three markers and players line up one behind the other behind the starting line or base.
▶ Player 1 takes a marker, runs to the first line, puts down the marker and runs back to base.
▶ Player 1 repeats with the second marker to the second line and the third marker to the third line.
▶ Player 2 repeats the process in reverse, by bringing the markers back to base, and so on; the winning team is the first to get all players back to base.

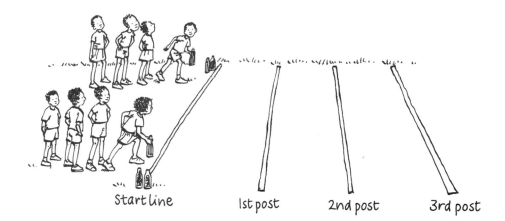

Start line   1st post   2nd post   3rd post

To make the activity easier:
▶ make the distances shorter
▶ play without the markers, students should touch the lines with their foot.

To make the activity harder:
▶ make the distances longer
▶ introduce an activity, for example a jump, before students pick up/put down the markers
▶ change the course, for example put the markers into a fan shape around the start line.

Teaching points

Ask the students
▶ **How can you turn quicker?**
  Pick up or put down the marker as you turn.
  Bend your knees to pick up/put down.

Stage 2 *Hopping*

Objectives
To teach students how to hop on both legs and to help them develop leg power, balance and co-ordination.

Equipment
One stick, to:
▶ mark lines on the ground for starting and finishing points 20 m apart (for Activities 1, 3, 4 and 5)
▶ mark squares on the ground, approximately 50 cm × 50 cm (for Activities 2 and 5)
▶ mark a line (Activity 3).

Safety
▶ Students should keep their distance from each other.

Activities

1 Hop on one leg from the starting line to the finishing line. Then hop back to the starting line on the other leg.

2 Stand in one of the four squares and hop on one leg around the square, first clockwise, then anti-clockwise. Change legs and repeat.

3 Hop along a straight line on one leg, landing on alternate sides of the line. Return using other leg.

4 Hop on one leg, put weight onto the other leg and then hop on that leg. Repeat the hopping and skipping on alternate legs to the line and back.

5 Hop on one leg and land with feet apart. Repeat this to the line and back.

To make the activities easier:
▶ make the distances shorter
▶ change legs more frequently; for example change legs after three hops in Activity 1.

To make the activities more difficult:
▶ make distances longer
▶ change legs less often; for example use one leg only to go back and forth in Activity 1.

Activities 1, 3, 4 and 5 can also be made competitive by grouping students into teams and having relay races.

Teaching points

Ask the students
▶ **How do you keep your balance?**
  Keep your head still, think tall and do not let your stomach sag.
▶ **How can you hop further or higher?**
  Push harder into the ground as you hop.
  Use your arms.

Stage 3 *Skipping*

Objectives
To teach students how to skip with a rope on their own and with others, in order to help them develop balance, timing and co-ordination.

Equipment
▶ Skipping ropes.
▶ Smooth surface.

Safety
▶ Students should keep their distance from each other by using grids.
▶ Do not try Activities 4, 5 and 6 until the students can master Activities 1, 2 and 3.
▶ Make sure the ropes are the right lengths for the students.

Wrong   Right

Activities
1 Jump with both feet together.

2 Jump using alternate legs.

3 Run and jump at the same time: jump the rope as you run.

4 Jump with both feet together, with arms and rope crossing over.

5 Jump in pairs. One student turns the rope while the other dodges the rope to jump face to face with their partner and at the same time.

6 Jump in groups. Two students turn the rope, while the others take turns to dodge the rope, jump it and move quickly out of the way as the next one begins. If students make an error, they change places with one of the students turning the rope.

To make the activities easier:
▶ take more time between skips by bouncing more times before turning the rope
▶ turn the rope more slowly.

To make the activities harder:
▶ turn the rope more quickly
▶ put in two turns of the rope to one skip; students will need to jump higher and turn the rope quicker to help them do this.

> ## Teaching points
>
> **Ask the students**
> ▶ **Where should the rope be as you jump?**
> Make the rope just skim the floor.
> ▶ **What can you do to help you keep to a rhythm?**
> Count as you jump, for example '1, 2, skip, 1, 2, skip ...'

Stage 4 *Jumping*

Objectives
To teach students the difference between jumping for height and for distance and to help develop power.

Equipment
▶ One stick to mark out lines and distances.
▶ One rope and two sticks (Activity 5); markers can be used instead.

Safety
▶ Try to find soft ground for students to jump on.
▶ Students should let their knees give on landing.

Activities
1 Stand with feet together and jump.

2 Jump with feet together over the markers.

3 Run and jump for length.

4 Run and jump for height.

5 Jump alternate sides of the rope.

wall or
stick

To make the activities easier:
▶ jump shorter distances and lower heights.

To make the activities harder:
▶ jump further and higher.

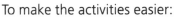

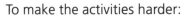

Teaching points

Ask the students
▶ **How can you jump higher or longer?**
Push harder into the ground as you jump.
▶ **What can you do to help you keep to a rhythm?**
Use your arms.

Stage 5 *Chasing and running away*

Objectives
To teach students how to run quickly and dodge others, whether they are attacking (running away) or defending (chasing).

Equipment
▶ Large playing area.
▶ Coloured bands for chasers.

Safety
▶ With very large groups, put students into smaller groups and mark off separate playing areas to avoid collisions.
▶ Students should look where they are going to anticipate and avoid collisions.

Activity
- ► Use a large space.
- ► Pick out approximately one in five students to be chasers; give them a coloured band to distinguish them from the others.
- ► When you say 'go', everyone tries to run away from the chasers. The chasers try to catch and touch those running away.
- ► Once the chasers have caught three people, the third one they catch becomes the new chaser: the chaser who catches the third person gives him or her their band, so everyone can see the new chaser. (The students who are caught first or second continue to run from the chasers.)

To make the activity easier for the chasers:
- ► give students less space in which to run away
- ► decrease the number of touches they must get before they exchange roles.

To make the activity more difficult for the chasers:
- ► give students more space in which to run away
- ► increase the number of people the chasers must catch before they are allowed to change roles.

Teaching points

Ask the students
- ► **What can you do to help you catch others or avoid being caught?**
  Use quick dodging movements.
  Anticipate the movements of the chaser or person running away.

Stage 6 *Running, jumping and reactions*

Objectives
To help students improve their reactions, speed and movements.

Equipment
- ► Open space.

Safety
- ► Students should keep their distance from each other.

Activity
- ▶ The students spread out in an open space, facing the teacher.
- ▶ The teacher runs in different directions and jumps in different ways.
- ▶ The class reacts immediately to the teacher's movements and copies them.

To make the activity easier:
- ▶ the teacher changes movements at regular intervals
- ▶ the teacher changes movements less frequently
- ▶ the teacher keeps movements simple, for example dodges left and right, jumps up.

To make the activity more difficult:
- ▶ the teacher changes movements at irregular intervals
- ▶ the teacher changes movements more frequently
- ▶ the teacher makes movements more complex, for example runs and jumps in all directions, hops and skips.

Teaching points

Ask the students
- ▶ **What can you do to help you keep up with the teacher?**
  Keep your eyes on the teacher at all times, react immediately to movements and keep your movements light so you can change movements or directions quickly.
- ▶ **How can you make your movements more positive and powerful?**
  Push harder into the ground with your legs as you move or change direction.

Volunteers and colleagues suggest that a similar activity can be used to develop netball skills specifically. Students should run around an area, for example a netball court. Blow the whistle once to indicate that students should stop and pivot before they continue to run. Blow the whistle twice to indicate that students should stop and change direction.

Throwing and catching skills

Throwing and catching skills help to develop timing and balance. These skills are essential for invasive games such as basketball, netball, handball and rugby. They are also necessary grounding for

See also page 15 for volunteers' and colleagues' recommendations for practices with larger numbers. Although these practices are outlined for hitting and kicking skills, they can also be used for passing and dribbling.

rounders, cricket, softball, volleyball and throwing skills such as javelin and shot put.

Stage 1 *On your own*

Objectives

To teach students how to throw and catch in different ways by introducing them to activities they can practise on their own.

Equipment

► Balls or equivalent. Please note that many items can be used for throwing and catching, such rolled up material or paper, providing there are no rough edges; obviously balls need to be used for Activities 1, 3 and 4. Bundles or stones can be used for Activity 5; stones must only be used for throwing and not catching.
► Quoits (a circular or square hoop) (Activity 6).
► Stand/sticks (Activity 6).
► Markers for grids.

Safety

► Students should stay in their own grid.
► Students should stay away from any obstacles, for example trees, rocky terrain and fencing.

Activities

1 Bounce the ball on the ground and catch the rebound.

2 Throw the ball upwards and catch.

3 Bounce the ball on the ground, and tap the rebound instead of catching.

4 Bounce the ball to rebound as high as possible and catch.

5 Mark a square on the ground or use a tub; throw the ball/stone/bean bag into the space or target.

6 Stand a stick or pole in the ground or on a stand; throw the quoits so they fall onto the target.

To make the activities easier:
- ► find smoother surfaces
- ► use a larger, softer ball
- ► stand close to targets or make them bigger (Activities 5 and 6)
- ► bounce or throw the ball closer to the body.

To make the activities more difficult:
- ► use a smaller, harder ball
- ► tap and bounce while walking or running to make the game more difficult (Activity 3)
- ► stand further from targets or make them smaller (Activities 5 and 6)
- ► bounce or throw the ball further or higher
- ► throw and catch with one hand only.

To make the activities competitive, count the number of targets or catches.

Teaching points

Ask the throwers
- ► **How can you control the throw?**
  Use a smooth arm/wrist/hand action, grip the ball loosely before releasing, and follow through towards the target.
- ► **How should you send the ball to make it easier/harder to catch?**
  Experiment with low, high, slow or fast throws.
- ► **With which foot do you step forward?**
  Step forward with the opposite foot to your throwing arm, so you are balanced and transfer your body weight.

Ask the catchers
- ► **How do you prepare to catch the ball?**
  Move your feet into position in line with the flight of the ball.
  Watch the ball closely.
- ► **How do you soften the impact?**
  Relax your hands and arms so they give and move with the ball.
  Pull your hands and arms in as the ball is received.

Stage 2 *In pairs*

Objectives
To help students learn how to throw and catch by introducing them to activities they can practise with a partner.

Equipment
- ► One ball per pair. Please note that many items can be used for throwing and catching, such as rolled up material or paper, providing there are no rough edges. If possible, encourage students to use different shapes and weights of balls or equivalent.
- ► Four markers per pair for grids.

Safety
- ► Students should stay in their own grid.
- ► Students should make sure their partner is ready before they throw.

Activities

1 Throw with the dominant hand and catch with both hands.

2 Throw and catch a rugby/uneven shaped ball with both hands.

3 Throw and catch alternate high and low throws.

4 Throw and catch while moving.

To make the activities easier:
► pairs stand close together
► use a larger, softer ball.

To make the activities more difficult:
► pairs stand further apart
► use a smaller, heavier ball
► throw and catch with one hand only
► throw overarm.

To make the activities competitive, count the number of consecutive throws and catches.

Teaching points

Ask the throwers
► **How do you vary the height (Activity 3)?**
Imagine you are throwing over or under something.
► **Where do you throw the ball if your partner is on the move (Activity 4)?**
Throw the ball to where your partner indicates; this should be in front of the moving player. (Note that if you throw to the body, the player will run past the ball.)

Ask the catchers
► **How can you be balanced for the catch?**
Move your feet into position in line with the flight of the ball and keep your feet apart.
► **How can you show where you want to catch the ball?**
Call or indicate with your hands where you want the ball.

Stage 3 *In pairs with targets*

Objectives
To help students learn how to throw and catch with accuracy.

Equipment

▶ One ball per pair. Please note that many items can be used for throwing and catching, such as rolled up material or paper, providing there are no rough edges. If possible encourage students to use different shapes and weights of balls or equivalent.
▶ Four markers per pair for grids.
▶ Two targets, one net, rope or targets (Activity 4).

Safety

▶ Students should stay in their own grid.
▶ Students should make sure their partner is ready before they throw.

Activities

1 Throw and catch, as one player moves closer and further away to vary the distance.

2 Throw and catch, as one player moves to one side to catch the ball, then the other.

3 Throw and catch, aiming to bounce the ball on the target.

4 Throw and catch over a rope, line or target.

To make the activities easier:
▶ pairs stand close together
▶ throwers throw the ball so the catchers can receive it at waist height.

To make the activities more difficult:
▶ pairs stand further apart
▶ throwers throw the ball so catchers must move quickly or catch the ball low or high

- throw and catch with one hand only
- alternate throws so catchers receive the ball before and after bounce (Activities 1, 2 and 4).

To make the activities competitive, count the number of consecutive throws and catches.

Teaching points

Ask the throwers
- **How do you vary direction/distance?**
  Follow through in the direction you want the ball to go.
- **How much space do you leave for the bounce?**
  Make a note of where the ball hits the ground and how far/where it bounces. (Note that the bounce should be approximately two-thirds of the distance between the players.)

Ask the catchers
- **What must you remember if you are letting the ball bounce?**
  Anticipate the pace, length and position of the bounce.
  Move quickly according to where the ball bounces and get behind the ball, allowing enough space for the bounce.

Stage 4 *In threes*

Objective
To help students learn how to throw, catch and intercept.

Equipment
- One ball per group of three. Please note that many items can be used for throwing and catching, such as rolled up material or paper, providing there are no rough edges. If possible encourage students to use different shapes and weights of balls or equivalent.
- Four markers per group for grids.
- One hoop (Activity 1).

Safety
- Students should stay in their own grid.
- Students should make sure their partner is ready before they throw.

Activities
1 Player 1 holds the hoop while Players 2 and 3 throw and catch through it.

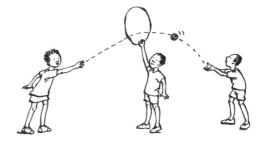

2 Player 1 stands with feet apart and arms stretched high. Players 2 and 3 roll the ball between Player 1's legs or throw it over the top of them.

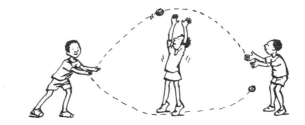

3 Player 1 stands in the middle and tries to catch the ball without moving the feet. Players 2 and 3 throw and catch, trying to prevent Player 1 from getting the ball.

4 Repeat Activity 3. Player 1 is also allowed to move and tries to anticipate the direction of the throw, react quickly and intercept the ball. Players can only move within their grid.

To make the activities easier for Player 1:
- ▶ keep the playing area/grid small
- ▶ Player 1 marks one player only, rather than standing an equal distance between the two
- ▶ Player 1 is only in the middle for a certain length of time.

To make the activities more difficult for Player 1:
- ▶ increase the playing area/grid
- ▶ Players 2 and 3 vary throws, move faster and dodge quicker.

Teaching points

Ask the throwers
- ▶ **How can you prevent Player 1 intercepting the ball (Activities 3 and 4)?**
  Try different ways of throwing, for example low/high/bounce throws; pretend to throw one way but then throw the other.

Ask the catchers
- ▶ **How can you get free and show your partner where you want the ball?**
  Watch the ball closely, look for space and use quick/dodging movements.

Let your partner know where you want the ball, for example by calling or indicating with your hand.
- ▶ **How does Player 1 stop the catcher from getting the ball?**
  Anticipate the moves and throws of Players 2 and 3.
  React and move quickly, and put pressure on Players 2 and 3 by moving towards them and marking their moves when they have the ball, and by marking their movements closely when they are trying to get free.

Teaching large classes

Volunteers and colleagues recommend this activity for large numbers.

Activity

Students are divided into two teams and stand either side of a centre line. A bench is placed behind each team. Throw approximately five balls into the playing area, either side of the centre line. Students are then free to roll the ball to the other side, aiming to hit below the knee of the opposing players or the bench behind them. If hit, students must stand out. If a player hits the bench of the opposing team, the members of that team must all freeze while the other team has one free throw. Teams aim to avoid the balls from the opposition hitting their legs and try to catch them. This will prevent the balls from hitting their own bench and means players can then aim to eliminate the players on the other team.

Hitting and kicking skills

Hitting (or striking) and kicking skills help to develop timing and balance. Throwing and catching games, and running and jumping games, will help students develop their hitting/striking and kicking skills. Hitting/striking skills are essential for hockey, volleyball, rounders, cricket and softball. Kicking skills are necessary for football and rugby.

Stage 1 On your own

Objectives

To teach students how to move with the ball (dribble) and kick, hit or push the ball by introducing them to activities they can practise on their own.

Equipment

One stick to draw a line, and one ball per player. Please note that many items can be used for these activities, such as rolled up material or paper (Activity 1).
▶ Five markers (Activity 2).
▶ Wall space or bench (Activity 3).

Safety

▶ Make sure students are well spaced, and put them into small groups.

Activities

1 Dribble along a line and return.

2 Dribble through markers and return.

3 Kick or hit the ball, or push the ball (with the stick or the foot starting in contact with the ball), against the wall or bench, and stop the rebound. Repeat.

To make the activities easier:
▶ dribble at a slower pace (Activities 1 and 2)
▶ place the markers further apart (Activity 2)
▶ stand close to the wall or bench and catch the rebound with the hands (Activity 3).

To make the activities more difficult:
▶ dribble at a faster pace (Activities 1 and 2)
▶ place the markers closer together (Activity 2)
▶ stand further from the wall or bench (Activity 3).

Teaching points

Ask the throwers
▶ **How can you keep control of the ball?**
Keep the ball close to your foot or stick, look where you are going, and only go as fast as you can control (Activities 1 and 2).

▶ **What can you do to help you stop the rebound?**
Watch the rebound closely and make sure your foot or stick is behind the ball.

Stage 2 *In pairs*

Objectives

To help students learn how to kick, hit or push the ball by introducing them to practices they can do in pairs.

Equipment

▶ One ball per pair. Please note that many items can be used for these activities, such as rolled up material or paper.
▶ Wall, bench space or barrier per pair.

Safety

▶ Make sure pairs are well spaced.

Activities

1 Player 1 kicks, hits or pushes the ball to Player 2. Player 2 stops the ball and returns. Repeat.

2 Player 1 kicks, hits or pushes the ball against a wall or barrier. Player 2 stops the ball and repeats.

3 Player 1 dribbles with the ball and then kicks, hits or pushes the ball to Player 2. Player 2 stops the ball, dribbles with the ball and returns to Player 1. Repeat.

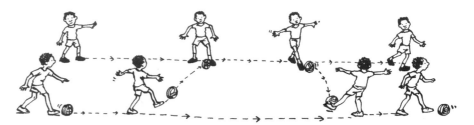

To make the activities easier:
- ▶ move closer to your partner or to the wall
- ▶ give yourself more time to control and pass the ball.

To make the activities more difficult:
- ▶ move further away from your partner or the wall.
- ▶ pass and dribble at a quicker pace.

Teaching points

Ask the students
- ▶ **How can you make your pass accurate?**
  Ensure you have control of the ball before you pass it.

- ▶ **Where should you pass to your partner (Activity 3)?**
  Pass the ball to where your partner indicates; this is usually in front of them so that they do not run past the ball.

Stage 3 *In pairs with targets*

Objectives
To help students learn how to kick, hit or push the ball by introducing them to practices they can do in pairs.

Equipment
- ▶ One ball per pair. Please note that many items can be used for these activities, such as rolled up material or paper.
- ▶ Two markers per pair (Activity 1).

▶ A wall, bench space or barrier per pair and target (Activity 2).
▶ Two sticks and some rope per pair (Activity 3).

Safety
▶ Make sure pairs are well spaced.

Activities
1 Players kick, hit or push the ball between the markers to each other.

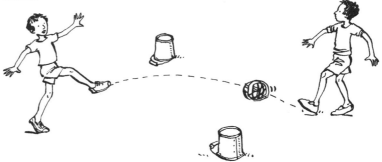

2 Player 1 kicks, hits or pushes the ball towards a target on the wall. Player 2 stops the rebound and returns the ball.

3 Player 1 kicks, hits or pushes the ball over or under the rope. Player 2 stops the ball and returns the ball to Player 1.

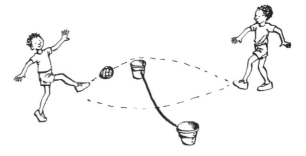

To make the activities easier:
▶ increase the target area.

To make the activities more difficult:
▶ decrease the target area.

Teaching points

Ask the students
▶ **How can you set yourselves realistic targets?**
  Set easy targets at first, then make them harder as you improve.

Stage 4 *In threes*

Objectives
To help students learn how to kick, hit or push the ball by introducing them to practices they can do in threes.

Equipment

▶ One ball per group. Please note that many items can be used for these activities, such as rolled up material or paper.

Safety

▶ Make sure groups are well spaced.

Activities

1 Player 1 kicks, hits or pushes the ball to Player 2. Player 2 stops the ball and passes to Player 3. Player 3 stops the ball and passes to Player 1.

2 Player 1 kicks, hits or pushes the ball to Player 2. Player 2 stops the ball and passes back to Player 1. Player 3 tries to intercept the passes.

3 Player 1 kicks, hits or pushes the ball to Player 2. Player 2 stops the ball and passes to Player 3. Player 3 stops the ball and passes to Player 2. Player 2 stops the ball and passes to Player 1.

To make the activities easier:
▶ move and pass the ball more slowly
▶ stand closer to the other players in your group.

To make the activities more difficult:
▶ move and pass the ball at a faster pace
▶ stand further away from the other players in your group.

Teaching points

Ask the students

▶ **What can you do to ensure that the ball keeps moving and everyone benefits from the exercise (Activities 1 and 3)?**
Co-operate with others in the group; you should not deliberately pass the ball so others cannot reach or control it.

▶ **How can you get the ball past Player 3 (Activity 2)?**
Use quick dodging movements to encourage Player 3 to go the wrong way; this will give you more free space to pass the ball.

Teaching large classes

Volunteers and colleagues recommend these practices if equipment is severely restricted and you are teaching large classes.

The following practices can be used for activities such as netball, basketball and volleyball, as well as for hockey and football.

Students find a partner and line up facing each other, approximately 5 m from their partner, and 2 m from the pair next to them. Students hit or kick the ball to the next player in the group. The ball travels down the group to the end and then back again in the opposite direction. Where there is movement, when players are dribbling the ball to the next player, players stay in their new position until the ball comes to them and they move again.

• • •

Students are divided into two teams. The first person in the team hits or kicks the ball to the first person in the opposite team and then either joins the back of their own team or the opposite team.

Session plan

See pages 9–12 for examples of two progressive session plans, which include activities for throwing and catching games.

6

Invasive games

By the end of this chapter, you will be able to teach invasive games. Invasive games share many similar skills, and the activities in this chapter help students to develop and practise these skills. The chapter then lists the rules for mini and full games of basketball, handball, netball, football, hockey and rugby.

Introduction

Invasive games are grouped together because they all involve two competing teams who have to defend their own territory and goal, and attack their opponent's territory and goal. The aim of invasive games is to score a goal or a try. Since invasive games have the same aim, they also require many of the same skills. That is why it is helpful to teach the skills for these games together. The skills and tactics needed, for example, to pass the ball or dodge a defender, can be transferred to many different games.

The skills needed to play invasive games include throwing, catching, running, kicking and hitting. The activities in this chapter help children to develop these skills and build on the basic sports skills described in Chapter 4.

In invasive games, players have different responsibilities within teams, and in some games they have restrictions on where they are allowed to play. Invasive games require individual skills such as scoring goals, as well as a strong emphasis on team play and tactics. Do not be tempted to introduce students to the full games of the different sports before you have worked through the mini games. This is because students have more opportunity in mini games to practise their skills because there are generally less people involved in a smaller playing area. As a result they are far more likely to enjoy the games and improve their skills.

This chapter is divided into three main sections, which cover the three types of invasive games:
- ▶ **goal-throwing games** where a goal is scored by throwing the ball; these games include basketball, netball and handball
- ▶ **goal-striking games** where a goal is scored by striking the ball without using the arms; these games include football and hockey
- ▶ **try-scoring games** where a try rather than a goal is scored by carrying the ball over a line, rather than striking or throwing it into a goal; these games include rugby.

Within each section, general activities first develop the skills that students need to play all or some of the games in that section. This leads on to the specific games: the rules for both the mini and full versions of each game are fully explained. The metric measurements for the pitch and equipment are the official ones stipulated in the rules of each sport. If space and resources are limited, you should feel free to improvise and make the best of what is available.

Goal-throwing games

There are two types of goal-throwing games. The first is when the person with the ball is restricted in terms of movement. For example for netball, you are only allowed to take one step, from your landing foot, before you throw the ball; you are not allowed to run or dribble with the ball. The second type allows movement with the ball. For example, in basketball and handball you are allowed to dribble with the ball.

Stage 1 *Moving and passing*

Volunteers and colleagues have found this game particularly useful because it can include large numbers but only requires one netball.

Objectives
To help students learn how to move and pass the ball to each other, in different directions, and to help them improve speed and accuracy.

Equipment
▶ One ball.

Safety
▶ Students should look where they are going as well as at the ball.
▶ Students should not pass the ball if they think the player they are throwing to is not looking and will be hit.

Activity
▶ Divide the class into four equal teams and name them A, B, C and D.
▶ Line up the students so that Team A faces Team C and Team B faces Team D.

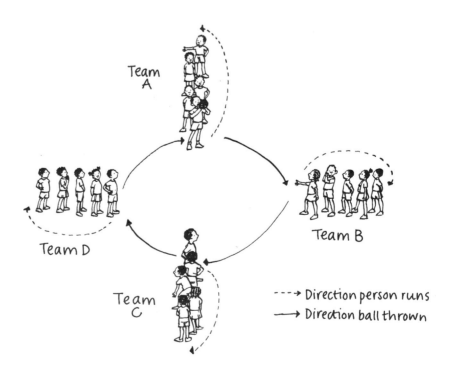

- The front player in Team A passes the ball slightly in front of the player in Team B, who catches it and then passes to the front player from Team C. Please note that for netball, you should encourage students to practise accurate footwork at all times.
- After catching and passing the ball, players run to the back of their team and wait for their next turn.
- The game continues until each player has had at least two turns.

To make the activity easier:
- teams stand closer together
- players throw more slowly and take more time between throws.

To make the activity more difficult:
- teams stand further apart
- players receive and pass the ball more quickly.

The game can be made competitive by teams losing a 'life' if they drop a catch or throw inaccurately: the team with the least number of lives lost by the end of the game is the winner.

Teaching points

Ask the students
- **How can you avoid dropping the ball?**
  Concentrate so you know exactly when it is your turn to throw and catch, who you are throwing to, and who is throwing to you.
  Pass at a comfortable pace for everyone in the group.

Stage 2 *Dribbling*

Objective
To teach students how to dribble the ball.

Equipment
- One ball per team.
- Four markers per team.

Safety
- Keep teams well spaced.

Activity
- Group students into teams of three to five.
- Player 1 runs in and out of the markers to the line and back, while bouncing the ball.
- Player 1 passes the ball to the next player in line.
- Players repeat the actions of Player 1 in turn and the winning team is the first one to get all players back to the start.

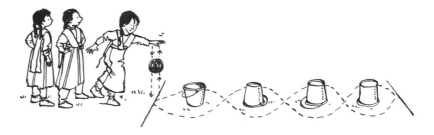

To make the activity easier:
► put the markers further apart
► use your dominant hand only.

To make the activity more difficult:
► put the markers closer together
► use your non-dominant hand
► change your dribbling hand each time you go round the marker.

Teaching points

Ask the students
► **How can you keep control of the ball as you run?**
Keep the ball in front and close to you.
Look where you are going.

Stage 3 *Shooting and catching the rebound*

Objectives
To help students learn how to shoot accurately and to retrieve the ball if it rebounds.

Equipment
► One ball per team.
► One goalpost and one backboard (optional) per team. Two teams may use the same goalpost if necessary.
► Approximately three markers to indicate the position from which players may shoot.

Safety
► If two teams are using the same goalpost, players should take turns to shoot.

Activity
► Group students into teams of three to five.
► Player 1 shoots, catches the rebound, collects the ball, turns and passes the ball to Player 2.
► Player 2 repeats and passes to Player 3.
► Each team gets one point for scoring a goal with the use of the backboard and two points for scoring a goal without the use of the backboard. The winning team is the one that scores the most points.

Shots may either be taken from a certain point, for example as in netball, or players may dribble the ball closer to the net, take two steps closer to the goal and jump from one leg when attempting to score (lay up), as in basketball.

To make the activities easier:
▶ make the ring larger and lower
▶ stand closer to the ring
▶ shoot from the same place every time.

To make the activities more difficult:
▶ stand further from the ring
▶ shoot from different places every time.

Teaching points

Ask the students
▶ **How do you make use of the backboard when shooting?**
Aim for target on the backboard.
▶ **What must you remember on a lay up (basketball)?**
Jump high so you release the ball at the maximum height.

Stage 4 *Shooting and defending*

Objectives
To teach students how to score goals for handball and how to defend the goal.

Equipment
▶ One ball per group.
▶ One goal, made of two posts, and preferably a net or some barrier to stop the ball.
▶ A playing area in front of the goal with a semi-circle marked out.

Safety
▶ Do not throw until the goalkeeper is ready.
▶ Use soft ground if possible.

Activity
▶ Group students into teams of four to five.
▶ Each team has one goal to shoot towards, one person who is responsible for guarding the goal and preventing goals being scored (a goalkeeper), and one person who stands behind the goal to collect the ball if it goes past or misses the goalkeeper (a ball collector).
▶ Player 1 takes up to three steps towards the goal, remaining outside the semi-circle, and tries to score a point by throwing the ball past the goalkeeper and into the goal. Player 1 runs to the back of the queue.

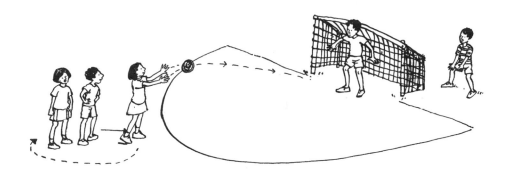

- ► The goalkeeper or ball collector passes the ball to Player 2 and Player 2 repeats.
- ► Shooters have five attempts at scoring a goal before the players change roles. Players count the number of goals they score.

To make the activity easier for the shooters:
- ► increase the size of the goal
- ► make the semi-circle smaller so you can shoot closer to the goal
- ► practise without goalkeepers.

To make the activities more difficult for the shooters:
- ► decrease the size of the goal
- ► make the semi-circle larger so that you have to shoot from further away.

Teaching points

Ask the goalkeepers
- ► **How do you put pressure on the shooter?**
Move forwards towards the shooter; this reduces shooting possibilities and gives you the best chance of intercepting the ball.
- ► **Can you predict where the ball will go?**
Sometimes you can tell, for example by the position of the shooter's body or the direction of their eyes, where the shooter is likely to aim. Usually this happens too quickly and you simply have to react and move immediately you know where the shot is going.

Ask the shooters
- ► **How can you give yourself a better chance?**
Pretend to throw in one direction so that the goalkeeper moves to cover this, leaving a space on the other side. This is wrong-footing the goalkeeper.
- ► **How can you improve your shooting skills?**
Experiment with different throws, for example different paces and directions.

Volunteers and colleagues suggest the numbers game (see pages 80–81) as an alternative if there are large numbers in your class. The following pre-game exercises help students prepare and improve their footwork skills for netball.

▶ To improve balance and stability, students stand on one leg and raise the other leg either in front or behind. When they are balanced in this position, instruct them to bend the knee of their supporting leg and slowly straighten it. They should repeat this a few times on each leg.

▶ To improve quick stopping movements without infringing the footwork rule, without taking more than one step, students begin running and at the sound of a command or whistle, they try to stop immediately without dragging their back foot forward. They then pivot 180 degrees on the landing foot and run in the opposite direction until the next command or whistle.

Stage 5 *2 versus 2*

Objectives
To help students think about the tactics of goal-throwing games and to help them improve their attacking and defending skills.

Equipment
▶ One ball per group.
▶ Markers for the playing area.
▶ Markers for a scoring point, for example a netball post, mini goal net, marker to touch with the ball.

Safety
▶ Make sure players remain in their own playing areas.
▶ Enforce the rule of players not being allowed to get in the way of or touch each other (do not make contact with each other).

Activity
▶ Group students into pairs of 2 versus 2 (preferably mixing girls and boys).
▶ One team starts with the ball and the player with the ball throws it from a centre mark within the playing area to start the game.
▶ The players/team with the ball aim to keep possession of it while moving towards their goal or scoring point. Their aim is to score a goal or make the ball touch the scoring point.
▶ The opposing players try to intercept the passes or goal shots and score goals at their scoring end.
▶ The game can be played as for netball, where players can only take one step in any direction when they have the ball; as for basketball, where players can only take one step in any direction when they have the ball but are allowed to run with the ball if they are dribbling; or as for handball, where players are allowed to move up to three steps with the ball and run with the ball if they are dribbling.

Scoring point

To make the activity easier:
▶ increase the size of the scoring point or goal.

To make the activity more difficult:

► decrease the size of the scoring point or goal
► increase the size of the playing area and group students into games of 3 versus 3 or 4 versus 4.

Teaching points

Ask the students

► **How do you keep possession of the ball?**
Get into a free space and let your partner/team know where you want the ball, for example by pointing or calling.

► **How do you take the ball away from the other team?**
Mark the movements of the opposition very closely.
Anticipate where the throw will go so you can intercept.

Rules for mini basketball

Equipment
► One basketball (approximately 22 cm).
► Two hoops/goalposts with backboards (see page 21 for how to make equipment). The height of the hoops/goalposts should be 2.6 m above the ground and their diameter should be 0.45 m. The backboards should be 1.08 m wide and 1.05 m high.
► A court with the correct measurements and markings (see below).

Aim of the game
The aim is to score more points than the opposing team by:
► scoring in the basket you are attacking
► stopping the opponents from scoring in the basket you are defending.

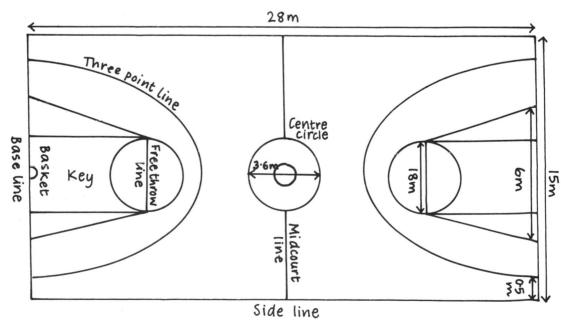

Court measurements and markings for mini basketball and basketball

Starting the game

The game starts with a 'jump ball' in the centre of the court. This is when a player from each team stands in the centre circle, and the referee throws the ball up above the heads of the two opposing players, who attempt to tap it to their team mates. Each player may touch the ball twice to tap it out of the circle. All the other players must be outside the centre circle. The game then continues with each team trying to gain or keep possession of the ball. Players may throw the ball to each other and take one step in any direction when they have the ball. They may run with the ball while dribbling.

Scoring

Points are scored every time a player successfully throws the ball into the basket. Two points are awarded for a basket scored in open play and one point for every basket scored from a penalty shot.

When a basket is scored, the game restarts with the other team passing the ball from the baseline.

Players

Each team consists of five players who play as attackers and defenders.

When the ball goes out-of-bounds

The game stops when the ball goes out-of-bounds and restarts with a pass from the side line. The team that last touched the ball loses possession. The other team passes the ball in from the side line.

Fouls

A foul is called when a player:
► blocks, holds or trips an opposing player
► charges into a defender who is stationary
► reaches over and makes contact with a ball handler in an attempt to steal the ball.

If a foul is committed, the other team is awarded a throw from the side line. If a foul is committed on a player attempting to shoot, the player is awarded two penalty shots (two attempts at goal without defence) from the free throw line.

Other

Other actions that are not allowed are:
► **double dribble** resuming dribbling (bouncing the ball) after stopping, or dribbling with both hands at the same time
► **travelling** taking more than one step while holding the ball, without dribbling it
► **3 seconds in key** an offensive player (the team/player in possession of the ball) is in the key (see diagram on page 63) for 3 consecutive seconds.

All of the above violations result in a side line throw to the other team.

Time

A game of mini basketball consists of four quarters each lasting 10 minutes. Teams change ends at the end of the second quarter.

Rules for basketball

Equipment

▶ One basketball.
▶ Two hoops/goalposts with backboards (see page 21 for how to make equipment). The backboards should be 1.08 m wide and 1.05 m high, with the lower edges 2.9 m above the ground. The hoops should be 3.05 m above the ground and their diameter should be 0.45 m.
▶ A court with the correct markings and measurements (the same as mini basketball).

Aim of the game

The aim is to score more points than the opposing team by:
▶ scoring in the basket you are attacking
▶ stopping the opponents from scoring in the basket you are defending.

Starting the game

The game starts with a 'jump ball' in the centre of the court. A player from each team stands in the centre circle and the referee throws the ball up above the heads of the two opposing players, who attempt to tap it to their team mates. All the other players must be outside the centre circle. The game then continues with each team trying to gain or keep possession of the ball. Players may throw the ball to each other and take one step in any direction when they have the ball. They may run with the ball while dribbling.

Scoring

Points are scored every time a player successfully throws the ball into the basket. Two points are awarded for a basket scored in open play, three points for a basket scored in open play from behind the three-point line and one point for every basket scored from a penalty shot.

When a basket is scored, the game restarts with the other team passing the ball from the baseline.

Player positions

Each team consists of five players who play as attackers and defenders. The three main positions are as follows:
▶ **guards** who play farthest from their attacking basket and are best at dribbling (bouncing) the ball; teams play with two guards
▶ **forwards** who play nearer their attacking basket and are the best shooters; teams play with two forwards
▶ **centres** who move the ball around the basket for shots and

catch rebounds; they make it difficult for the other team to score; teams play with one centre.

When the ball goes out-of-bounds
The game stops when the ball goes out-of-bounds and restarts with a pass from the side line. The team that last touched the ball loses possession. The other team passes the ball in from the side line.

Fouls
A foul is called when a player:
- blocks, holds or trips an opposing player
- charges into a defender who is stationary
- reaches over and makes contact with a ball handler in an attempt to steal the ball.

If a foul is committed, the other team is awarded a throw from the side line. If the foul is committed on a player attempting to shoot, the player is awarded two penalty shots (two attempts at goal without defence) from the free throw line. Any player who commits five fouls in a match is disqualified.

Other
Other actions that are not allowed are:
- **double dribble** resuming dribbling after having stopped, or dribbling with both hands at the same time
- **over-and-back** the attacking team returning the ball to the back half of the court after it has been passed or dribbled over the centre line
- **travelling** taking more than one step with the ball, without dribbling
- **3 seconds in key** an offensive player is in the key (see diagram on page 63) for 3 consecutive seconds
- **5 seconds in possession** holding the ball for 5 seconds when guarded by an opposing player within 6 ft
- **10 seconds in backcourt** the offensive team hold ball in backcourt for 10 seconds.

All of the above violations result in a side line throw to the other team.

Time
Basketball can be played in either two halves of 20 minutes each, or four quarters of 10 minutes each. There is usually an interval after the first half, or after each quarter.

Teams change ends at half-time or after two quarters, so that they are attacking the other basket.

Rules for mini handball

Equipment
▶ One handball (see pages 19–20 for how to make equipment). The ball should be about 15 cm in diameter.
▶ Two goals, one at each end of the pitch. Goals consist of two posts, 2.4 m apart and 1.6 m high, and these should be joined together with a cross-bar.
▶ A pitch with the correct measurements and markings.

Court measurements and markings for mini handball

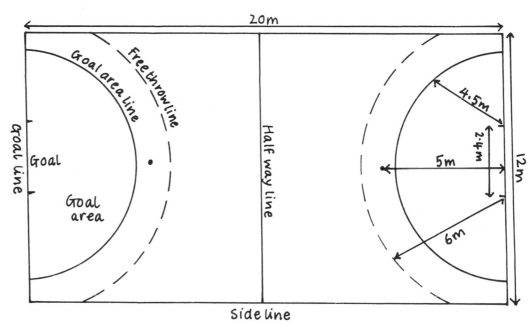

Aim of the game
The aim of mini handball is to score more goals than the opposing team by:
▶ scoring in the goal you are attacking
▶ stopping the opponents from scoring in the goal you are defending.

Starting the game
One team starts with the ball. The attacking team lines up on the half way line and moves forward to the opposing goal. The defending team defends the goal.

Scoring
A goal is scored every time a player successfully throws the ball into the net. One goal is awarded to the offensive team. The winner is the team with the most goals at the end of the game.

Players
Each team has five players consisting of four outfield players and a goalkeeper. Only the goalkeeper is allowed inside the goal area. The goalkeeper may move with the ball without restrictions, but may not carry the ball outside the goal area. Players are allowed to

hold the ball for up to 3 seconds, move up to three steps with the ball and run with the ball if they are dribbling it.

When the ball goes out-of-bounds

The game stops when the ball goes out-of-bounds and restarts with one of the following:

▶ A **throw-in** is taken when the ball goes out along the side line. The team that last touched the ball loses possession and the other team throws the ball in from behind the line where the ball went out of play.

▶ A **corner throw** is taken when a team causes the ball to go over its own goal line. The other team takes a free throw from the corner of the court.

▶ A **goal throw** is taken when a team causes the ball to go out along the goal line it is attacking. The goalkeeper of the other team takes a goal throw from within the goal area.

Fouls

A foul is called when a player:

▶ holds, trips, pushes, obstructs or kicks an opponent
▶ snatches the ball from an opponent
▶ touches the ball below the knee
▶ holds the ball for more than 3 seconds
▶ takes more than three steps when holding the ball, without bouncing it.

If a foul is committed, a free throw is awarded to the other team.

Penalty throws

A penalty throw is awarded to the attacking team when a:

▶ foul is committed that deprives a player of a scoring opportunity
▶ player illegally enters the goal area for defensive purposes.

A penalty throw is taken from the 5 m line in front of the centre of the goal, by the player who has been fouled.

Time

A game of mini handball consists of two halves lasting 10 minutes. At half time, teams change ends so that they are attacking the other end for the second half.

Rules for handball

Equipment

▶ One handball (see pages 19–20 for how to make equipment). The ball should weigh between 425 g and 475 g and have a circumference between 58 cm and 60 cm.

▶ Two goals, one at each end of the pitch. Goals consist of two posts, 3 m apart and 2 m high, and these should be joined together with a cross-bar.

▶ A pitch with the correct measurements and markings.

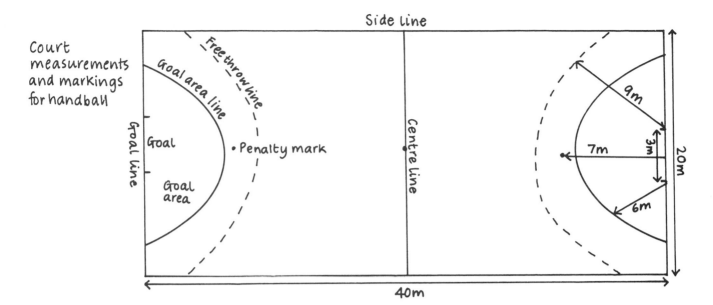

Court measurements and markings for handball

Aim of the game

The aim of handball is to score more goals than the opposing team by:
► scoring in the goal you are attacking
► stopping the opponents from scoring in the goal you are defending.

Starting the game

One team starts with the ball. The player with the ball passes from the centre of the court to start the game. Before the ball is thrown, teams must be in their own halves and all opposing players must be at least 3 m away from the player taking the throw.

Scoring

A goal is scored every time a player successfully throws the ball into the goal. One goal is awarded to the offensive team. The winner is the team with the most goals at the end of the match.

Players

Each team has seven players consisting of six outfield players and a goalkeeper. The goalkeeper is the only player allowed within the goal area. The goalkeeper may move with the ball without restrictions, but may not carry the ball outside the goal area. Players are allowed to hold the ball for up to 3 seconds, move up to three steps with the ball and run with the ball if they are dribbling it.

When the ball goes out-of-bounds

Play stops when the ball goes out-of-bounds and restarts with one of the following.
► A **throw-in** is taken when the ball goes out along the side line. The team who last touched the ball loses possession. The ball is thrown in by the other team from behind the line where the ball went out of play.

► A **corner throw** is taken when a team causes the ball to go out along its own goal line. The other team takes a free throw from the corner of the court.
► A **goal throw** is taken when a team causes the ball to go out along the goal line it is attacking. The goalkeeper of the other team takes a goal throw from within the goal area.

Fouls
A foul is called when a player:
► holds, trips, pushes, obstructs or kicks an opponent
► snatches the ball from an opponent
► touches the ball below the knee
► holds the ball for more than 3 seconds
► takes more than three steps when holding the ball, without bouncing it
► touches the ball more than once without it touching the ground, another player or part of the goal
► deliberately plays the ball out-of-bounds.

If a foul is committed, a free throw is awarded to the other team.

Penalty throws
A penalty throw is awarded to the attacking team when a:
► foul is committed that deprives a player of a scoring opportunity
► player illegally enters the goal area for defensive purposes.

A penalty throw is taken from the 5 m line in front of the centre of the goal, by the player who has been fouled.

Time
A game of handball consists of two halves, each lasting 30 minutes. At half time, teams change ends so that they are attacking the other end for the second half.

Rules for mini netball

Equipment
► One ball (see pages 19–20 for how to make equipment).
► Two goalposts, one at each end of the pitch. Their height should be between 2.43 m and 3.05 m.
► Each player should wear a bib showing their position (see page 22 for how to make bibs).
► A court with the correct markings.

Aim of the game
Players use their hands to pass the ball to their team mates. The aim is to score more goals than the opposing team by:
► scoring in the net you are attacking
► stopping the opponents from scoring in the net you are defending.

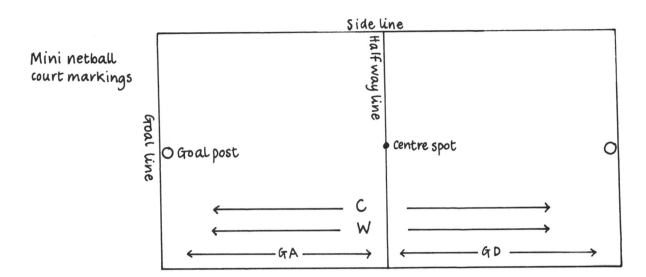

Starting the game

The game begins with the ball being thrown up between the Centres from each team on the mid-point of the half way line. The team who gains possession takes the first centre pass to start the game.

At each centre pass, the Goal Attacks and Goal Defenders may be anywhere in their half. The Wings must be in the attacking half. Players must be at least 2 m away from the Centre taking the pass, except for the opposing Centre who must be at least 1 m away (see under Player positions). Players are only allowed to move up to one step with the ball before it must be released and must always keep a distance of 1 m from the player with the ball.

Scoring

A goal is scored every time a team successfully throws the ball into the net. All players except the Goal Defenders are allowed to shoot. When a goal is scored, play restarts with a centre pass. Teams are given alternate centre passes.

Player positions

Each team has four players: Goal Attack (GA), Goal Defence (GD), Centre (C) and Wing (W). Centres and Wings are allowed anywhere on court. Goal Attacks may only play in their attacking half. Goal Defenders are only allowed in their defending half.

At half time, players swap positions. Centres swap with Wings and Goal Attacks swap with Goal Defenders.

When the ball goes out-of-bounds

When the ball goes out of the playing area, the team who last touched the ball loses possession. The other team has a free pass from behind the line where the ball went out of play.

Fouls

A foul is called when a player:
- kicks, strikes, bounces or falls on the ball
- holds the ball for 5 seconds
- impedes a player attempting to shoot
- loses and regains possession without the ball touching another player
- gets in an offside position (see Glossary).

All fouls result in a free pass to the other team, from where the foul took place. There are three types:
- **free pass** if the foul does not include body contact
- **penalty pass** if there is body contact; for a penalty the offender must stand by the side of the attacker, while the attacker has a free pass
- **penalty pass or shot** if there is a contact foul while shooting; this means the offender must stand by the side of the attacker, who can either pass or have a free shot at goal, providing they are inside the semi-circle.

Time

A game of mini netball consists of two halves, each lasting 15 minutes. Teams change ends after the first half.

Rules for netball

Equipment

For netball you need a ball and two posts. Each player wears a bib showing their position (see page 22 for how to make bibs).
- One ball (see pages 19–20 for how to make equipment). This should be between 690 mm and 710 mm in circumference and between 400 g and 450 g in weight.
- Two goalposts. Their height should be 3.05 m and the ring should be 380 mm in diameter (see page 21 for how to make equipment).
- A court with the correct measurements and markings.

Aim of the game

Players use their hands to pass the ball to their team mates. The aim is to score more goals than the opposing team by:
- scoring in the net you are attacking
- stopping the opponents from scoring in the net that you are defending.

Starting the game

One team starts with the ball and takes the first centre pass. The Centre of the starting team attempts to pass the ball from the centre circle to a team mate who must receive the ball within the centre third of the court. Only the Centres are allowed in the middle third until the game starts (see under Player positions). Players are only allowed to move up to one step with the ball

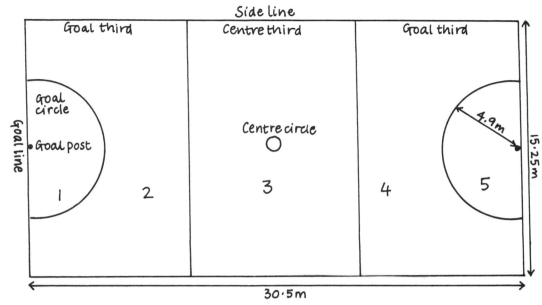

Court measurements and markings for netball

before it must be released, and must always keep a distance of 1 m from the player with the ball.

Scoring
A goal is scored every time a team successfully throws the ball into the net. A goal can only be scored by the Goal Shooter or Goal Attack of each team from within the attacking semi-circle.

When a goal is scored, play restarts with a Centre from the team whose turn it is.

Player positions
Each team has seven players. Each position has a restricted playing area. The positions and the areas of play (for a team attacking the goal on the left) are as follows (see diagram above):
▶ Goal Shooter, areas 1 and 2
▶ Goal Attack, areas 1, 2 and 3
▶ Wing Attack, areas 2 and 3
▶ Centre, areas 2, 3 and 4
▶ Wing Defence, areas 3 and 4
▶ Goal Defence, areas 3, 4 and 5
▶ Goalkeeper, areas 4 and 5.

When the ball goes out-of-bounds
When the ball goes out of the playing area, the team who last touched the ball loses possession. The other team has a free pass from behind the line where the ball went out.

Fouls
A foul is called when a player:
▶ kicks, strikes, rolls, bounces or falls on the ball
▶ holds the ball for 3 seconds
▶ loses and regains possession without the ball touching another player

- takes more than one step with the landing foot or feet before releasing the ball
- gets in an offside position (see Glossary)
- passes the ball over an entire third of the court.

All fouls result in a free pass to the other team, from where the foul took place. There are three types:
- **free pass** if the foul does not include body contact
- **penalty pass** if there is body contact; for a penalty the offender must stand by the side of the attacker, while the attacker has a free pass
- **penalty pass or shot** if there is a contact foul while shooting; the offender must stand by the side of the attacker, who can either pass or have a free shot at goal, providing they are inside the semi-circle.

Time
A game of netball consists of four quarters, each lasting 15 minutes. The teams change ends after each quarter.

Goal-striking games

Goal-striking games are used to help students learn the fundamental skills of sports such as hockey and football. Similar tactics apply to both these sports. Most of these games and skill exercises can be done either using the foot or a stick.

Optional practice for football only

Objective
To encourage players to use their heads in football.

Equipment
- One football per pair. Please note that only balls with a soft, smooth surface should be used.

Activity
- In pairs, Player 1 throws ball to Player 2, who heads the ball either upwards or downwards.
- The players repeat this 10 times and then change roles.
- When players progress they should try to keep the ball going. Both players should head the ball upwards to each other and count the number of consecutive passes.

Safety
- Students should mark out a grid and always remain in it.

Teaching points

Encourage the students to
► lean slightly backwards as the ball is approaching, with their neck held firmly, and then attack the ball with their head as they transfer their weight forwards.

Show the students
► how they should make contact with the ball in the middle of their forehead but adjust this slightly according to whether they are heading upwards (make contact with the ball slightly lower) or heading downwards (make contact with the ball slightly higher).

Stage 1 *Passing and intercepting*

Objectives
To help students learn how to pass to each other and to encourage them to intercept passes. Activities can help to develop football skills (by using footballs) or hockey skills (by using hockey sticks and balls).

Equipment
For hockey:
► One stick per player. If sticks are in short supply, you can play the game with one stick per group of three; Players 1 and 2 can roll the ball to each other, while Player 3 tries to intercept the ball with the stick.
► One ball per group of three.

For football:
► One football per group of three.

Safety
► Make sure groups are well spaced; mark out a space for each group.

Activity
► In groups of three, within a marked area, Players 1 and 2 pass to each other, avoiding Player 3.
► Player 3 tries to anticipate and stop the passes and counts the number of successful interceptions.
► Players change positions at the teacher's call.

To make the activity easier (for Player 3):

▶ mark out a small playing area for each group
▶ Players 1 and 2 can only touch the ball up to two times before they must pass.

To make the activity more difficult (for Player 3):

▶ mark out a large playing area for each group.

Teaching points

Ask Players 1 and 2
▶ **How can you avoid Player 3?**
Experiment with different ways of passing, for example pushing, flicking or hitting, and kicking; and different directions, for example passing to the left, to the right, through the legs.
Make Player 3 commit to moving one way so you have more free space; for example you might pretend you are passing right, wait until Player 3 moves to the right and then quickly pass to the left.
Communicate with your partners to let them know when, where and how you want the pass, for example by calling or indicating with hand.

Ask Player 3
▶ **How can you intercept the pass?**
Put pressure on the player with the ball by moving forwards to take the ball from the player in possession (tackling). This gives the player less time and less free space.

Preparation for the flick and the push. For the flick, move the stick underneath the ball

Preparation for the hit – the hands are closer together

A short, low pass

Preparation for a long pass. Move the foot underneath the ball for a high pass

Stage 2 *Dribbling and dodging players*

Objectives
To help students master the skill of getting past opponents while still maintaining possession of the ball, and to encourage them to intercept and challenge attackers.

Equipment
For hockey:
▶ Two sticks and two balls minimum per group of four.

For football:
▶ One football minimum per group of four.

Safety
▶ Make sure groups are well spaced.

Activity

▶ In groups of four (minimum), Player 1 dribbles (moves with the ball on the foot or the stick) forward to Player 2 and then passes the ball past Player 2. Player 1 then moves quickly past Player 2 and collects the ball.

▶ Player 2 tries to stop the ball but can only use the stick (their feet must stay still) or take one step in any direction.

▶ Player 1 continues dribbling with the ball to the far end and then Player 3 repeats the role of Player 1, trying to dribble and dodge Player 2, but runs in the opposite direction.

▶ When Player 3 reaches the end, Player 4 starts and so on; players who are dribbling count the number of times they pass Player 2 without being intercepted. Player 2 counts the number of times he or she successfully intercepted the ball.

▶ When all players have had two turns, players rotate positions.

To make the activity easier:
▶ replace Player 2 with a marker.

To make the activity more difficult:
▶ let Player 2 move as well as use the stick/foot for tackling.

Teaching points

Ask players with the ball
▶ **How can you dodge Player 2?**
Commit Player 2 to going one way so you have space to run past.
Experiment with different ways of getting past Player 2, for example by dodging one way and dribbling another; passing the ball one side of Player 2 and running the other; passing the ball through the legs of Player 2 and running past one side.
Use quick movements and run fast with the ball.

Stage 3 *Shooting and defending*

Objectives
To help attackers learn ways of getting past the goalkeeper to score goals, and to help the goalkeepers anticipate and prevent goals from being scored.

Equipment
▶ Markers for the goal and a line from which to score.

For hockey:
- ▶ Two sticks, one for the shooter and one for the goalkeeper, and one ball minimum per group.

For football:
- ▶ Two footballs minimum per group.

Safety
- ▶ Do not shoot until the goalkeeper is ready.
- ▶ In hockey do not let players lift their stick above shoulder height.

Activity
- ▶ In groups of four, each team has one goal, one goalkeeper and one ball collector.
- ▶ Player 1 in each team puts the ball on the line/marker and takes a shot at goal. Player 3 tries to stop the goal and passes the ball back to Player 1.
- ▶ Player 4 collects the ball if it goes past the goalkeeper and passes it back to Player 1, who collects it and goes to the back of the queue. Player 1 passes the ball to Player 2 if there is only one ball. Player 2 repeats.

- ▶ Players count the number of goals they score and goalkeepers count the number of goals they save in a given time.
- ▶ On the teacher's call, players change positions.

To make the activity easier for the shooters:
- ▶ increase the goal area
- ▶ practise first without the goalkeepers
- ▶ make the scoring line close to the goal.

To make the activity more difficult for the shooters:
- ▶ decrease the goal area
- ▶ make the scoring line further from the goal.

Teaching points

Ask the shooters
▶ How can you beat the goalkeeper?
Use quick, dodging movements to get goalkeeper to commit to going one way so you have space to score.
Experiment with different types of shot, for example push to the right, flick to the left, strong hit or kick through the legs.

Ask goalkeepers
▶ How can you save the goal?
Move forwards towards the shooter; this puts pressure on the shooter, reducing time and space.
▶ How can you predict where the ball will go?
Sometimes you can tell, for example by the position of the body, the foot or the stick, where the shooter is likely to aim, but often movements are so fast you can only react and move immediately you think you know where the ball is going.

Stage 4 *Dribbling, shooting and defending*

Objectives
To help students learn the skills of shooting on the run, and to develop further their ability as goalkeepers to prevent goals from being scored.

Equipment
▶ Approximately eight markers.

For hockey:
▶ Three sticks and two balls per group.

For football:
▶ Two footballs per group.

Safety
▶ Players dribbling the ball back to base must keep their distance from the player dribbling through the markers to the goal.
▶ In hockey, do not let players take their stick above shoulder height.

Activity
▶ In groups of three minimum, Player 1 defends the goal at the far end.
▶ Player 2 dribbles the ball around the markers and then tries to score a goal. Player 1 tries to stop the goal, collects the ball and dribbles it back to base.
▶ Player 2 takes the place of Player 1 to defend the goal, as Player 3 dribbles and attempts to score.
▶ Players keep rotating and count the number of goals scored.

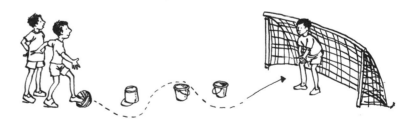

To make the activity easier for the attackers:
▶ make the goalkeepers stand behind the line so the attackers have a free shot at goal
▶ space the markers further apart.

To make the activity more difficult for the attackers:
▶ encourage the goalkeepers to tackle the attacker
▶ use more markers and keep them close together.

Teaching points

See also page 78 for Teaching points on shooting and defending.

Ask the students
► **When dribbling, how do you keep control of the ball?**
 Only go as fast as you can control.
 Keep the ball close to the stick or foot and stay close to the markers as you dribble around them.
 Keep your head up and look ahead, as well as at the ball.

Stage 5 *The Numbers Game*

Volunteers and colleagues particularly recommend this game as large numbers can be involved. Please note that this game may also be used for goal-throwing games instead of the 2 versus 2 game, to accommodate larger classes.

Objectives
To give students an opportunity to apply their skills to a game situation, and to help them experience the tactics involved in attacking and defending.

Equipment
► Mark out a rectangular area for play and mark the centre point. Put a goal or scoring point at each end, for example two markers for a goal or one marker that the ball must hit to score a goal.

For hockey:
► Five sticks per team minimum.
► One ball.

For football:
► One football.

Safety
► Make sure players remain in their own playing area.
► In hockey do not let players lift their stick above shoulder height.

Activity
► Divide the class into two teams, with each team standing either side of the area.
► Number each player on each team as shown on diagram.
► Call out numbers for either a 2 versus 2, 3 versus 3, 4 versus 4 or 5 versus 5 game. Each player called out runs to their own defending end and then runs to the middle.
► The first player to get to the middle can start the game by dribbling or passing the ball from the centre mark.
► Players try to keep possession of the ball, while moving towards their goal or scoring point.
► The attacking players aim to score a goal or make the ball touch the scoring point. The opposing players try to intercept the passes or goal shots, maintain possession of the ball and score goals at their own scoring end.

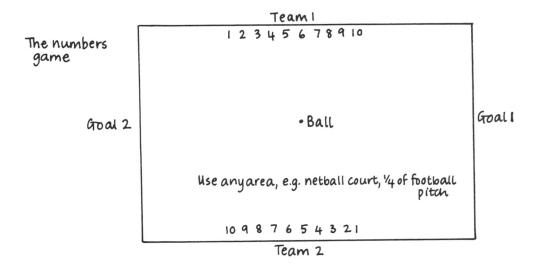

The numbers game

Team 1
1 2 3 4 5 6 7 8 9 10

Goal 2

• Ball

Goal 1

Use any area, e.g. netball court, ¼ of football pitch

10 9 8 7 6 5 4 3 2 1
Team 2

To make the activity easier:
▶ increase the size of the scoring point or goal.

To make the activity more difficult:
▶ decrease the size of the scoring point or goal
▶ restrict the number of passes allowed before the attacking players lose possession, for example if they fail to score a goal or point within 10 passes, the ball goes to the other team.

Teaching points

Ask the students
▶ **How do you keep possession of the ball?**
If a player on your team has the ball, move into a free space and let the player know where you want to receive the ball, for example by calling or pointing with your hand.

▶ **How do you get the ball from the other team?**
Mark the movements of the opposition very closely, and anticipate where they are passing or moving so you can intercept.
Communicate with your team, for example let them know where the ball or players are.

Rules for mini football

Equipment
▶ One ball.
▶ Two goals (3.66 m wide × 1.83 m high).
▶ A pitch with the correct markings.

Aim of the game
The aim of mini football is to score more goals than the opposing team by:
▶ scoring in the goal you are attacking
▶ preventing the opponents from scoring in the goal you are defending.

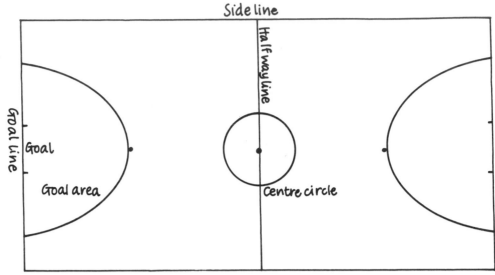

Pitch markings for mini football

Starting the game

One team starts with the ball. The game begins with one player passing the ball from the centre spot. This is called a kick-off.

Scoring

A goal is scored each time the ball crosses the goal line between the goalposts. The winner is the team with more goals at the end of the appointed time.

When a goal is scored the game restarts with a kick-off to the team that conceded the goal.

Players

Each team has five players consisting of a goalkeeper and four outfield players. The goalkeeper remains in the goal area to defend the goal and is the only player allowed to use their hands to touch the ball. The outfield players may not enter the goal area at any time but may play in any other area of the pitch.

When the ball goes out-of-bounds

The game stops when the ball goes out-of-bounds and restarts with one of the following.
- ▶ A **roll-in** is taken when the ball goes over the side line. The team who last touched the ball loses possession. The ball is rolled in by a member of the other team from behind the side line where the ball went out of play.
- ▶ A **corner pass** is taken when a team kicks the ball behind its own goal line. The other team then passes the ball from the corner.
- ▶ A **goal throw** is taken when a team kicks the ball behind the goal line it is attacking. The defending goalkeeper then throws the ball out.

Fouls

A foul is called when a player:

▶ pushes, obstructs, trips, kicks or holds an opposing player

▶ illegally touches the ball with the hand or lower arm

▶ kicks the ball above head height

▶ illegally enters the goal area.

If a dangerous foul is committed the player may be booked (cautioned). Players who are booked twice in a match are automatically sent off. Players who commit a very serious offence will be sent off without warning.

When a foul is committed the other team is awarded a free kick. It may be direct, where the team may shoot directly at goal, or indirect, where the ball must be touched by another player before a goal can be scored.

Penalty kicks

Penalty kicks are awarded to the attacking team if the defending goalkeeper handles the ball outside the goal area or if an outfield player touches the ball in the defending goal area. A free kick at goal is taken from the penalty spot with only the goalkeeper defending the shot.

Time

A game of mini football consists of two halves of equal length. They may last from 5 to 20 minutes each. At half time, the teams change ends so they are attacking the other goal for the second half.

Rules for football

Equipment

▶ One ball (approximately 55 cm in circumference).

▶ Two goals (7.32 m wide × 2.44 m high).

▶ A pitch with the correct markings.

Aim of the game

The aim is to score more goals than the opposing team by:

▶ scoring in the goal you are attacking

▶ preventing the opponents from scoring in the goal you are defending.

Starting the game

One team starts with the ball. The game begins with one player passing the ball from the centre spot (this is called a kick-off). Players must be in their own half of the field during the kick-off. The opposing team is not allowed in the centre circle during the kick-off.

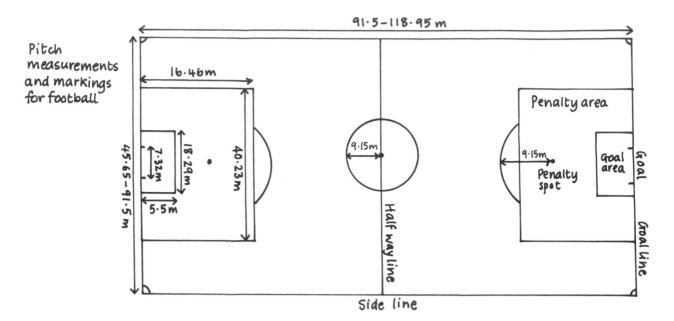

Pitch measurements and markings for football

91.5–118.95 m

16.46m

45.65–91.5 m

7.32m

18.24m

40.23m

5.5m

9.15m

Half way line

Penalty area

9.15m

Penalty spot

Goal area

Goal

Goal line

Side line

Scoring

A goal is scored each time the ball crosses the goal line between the goalposts. The winner is the team with more goals at the end of the appointed time.

When a goal is scored, the game restarts with a kick-off to the team that conceded the goal.

Player positions

Each team consists of 11 players. The four main positions are:
- **forwards** are mainly concerned with attacking play; teams play with one or two forwards
- **midfielders** play in the middle of the pitch and are concerned with attacking and defending; teams play with three to five midfielders
- **defenders** are concerned with preventing the other team from scoring; teams play with three to five defenders
- **goalkeepers** play in front of the goal they are defending and try to prevent the opposing team from scoring. The goalkeeper is the only player allowed to use hands to touch the ball within the goal area. Each team has one goalkeeper.

When the ball goes out-of-bounds

The game stops when the ball goes out-of-bounds and restarts with one of the following.
- A **throw-in** is taken when the ball goes over the side line. The team who last touched the ball loses possession and the ball is thrown in by a member of the other team from behind the side line where the ball went out of play.
- A **corner kick** is taken when a team kicks the ball behind its own goal line. The other team kicks the ball from the corner. Opposing players must be positioned at least 10 yards away from the player kicking the ball.
- A **goal kick** is taken when a team kicks the ball behind the goal

line it is attacking. The defending team takes a free kick from inside the goal box. Opposing players must be outside the penalty area when the kick is taken.

Fouls
A foul is called when a player:
- ▶ pushes, obstructs, trips, kicks or holds an opposing player
- ▶ illegally touches the ball with the hand or lower arm
- ▶ is in the offside position (see Glossary) when that team is attacking.

If a dangerous foul is committed, the player may be booked (cautioned). Any players booked twice in a match are automatically sent off. Any player who commits a very serious offence will be sent off without warning.

When a foul is committed the other team is awarded a free kick. It may be direct, where the team may shoot directly at goal, or indirect, where the ball must be touched by another player before a goal can be scored.

Penalty kicks
Penalty kicks are awarded to a team if they are fouled in the penalty area they are attacking. A free kick at goal is taken from the penalty spot, with only the goalkeeper defending the shot. All other players must be outside the penalty area when the kick is taken.

Time
A game of football consists of two halves of 45 minutes each. At half time, the teams change ends so they are attacking the other goal for the second half.

Rules for mini hockey

Equipment
- ▶ One ball (approximately 110 g).
- ▶ Two goals (3.65 m wide × 2.13 m high).
- ▶ One stick for each player (see page 20 for how to make equipment).
- ▶ A pitch with the correct measurements and markings.

Aim of the game
The aim is to score goals, using the hockey stick to hit the ball into the opponent's goal.

Starting the game
The game begins with one team passing the ball back from the centre spot. Teams must be in their own half of the field during the pass-back.

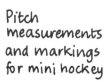

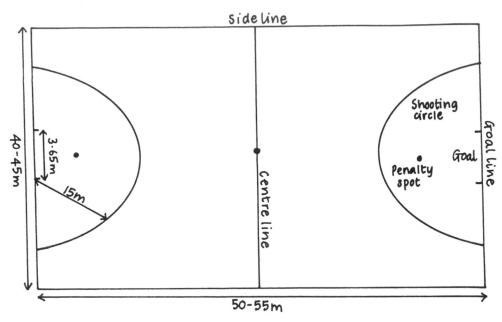

Pitch measurements and markings for mini hockey

40-45m

3.65m

15m

50-55m

side line

Shooting circle

Goal line

Goal

Penalty spot

centre line

Scoring

A goal is scored when a player successfully hits the ball into the goal, from within the goal circle. The winner is the team with more goals at the end of the match.

When a goal is scored, the game restarts with a pass-back to the team that conceded the goal.

When the ball goes out-of-bounds

The game stops when the ball goes out-of-bounds and restarts with one of the following.

▶ A **side line pass** is taken when the ball goes out along the side line. The team who last touched the ball loses possession and the ball is hit in by the other team from behind the line where the ball went out of play.

▶ A **goal hit** is taken when a team causes the ball to cross the goal line it is attacking. The defending team takes a free hit taken level with the top of the circle and opposite where the ball crossed the goal line.

▶ A **long corner** is taken when a team unintentionally causes the ball to cross its own goal line. The other team takes a free hit from the corner.

▶ A **penalty corner** is taken when a team intentionally causes the ball to cross its own goal line. The other team takes a free hit from the penalty corner mark.

When a penalty corner is taken, no players may be in the goal circle except for the defending goalkeeper. Up to five defending players may stand on the goal line and move into the goal circle when the ball is played.

Fouls

A foul is called when a player:

- touches the ball with any part of the body or anything other than the flat side of the stick (except for the goalkeeper who may use the hands and feet to control the ball)
- plays the ball in a dangerous way.

A foul committed in the attacking half of the pitch results in a free hit to the other team from where the foul took place. An intentional foul committed within the defending half, but outside the goal circle, results in a penalty corner to the other team. An unintentional foul committed within the defending goal circle results in a penalty corner to the other team. An intentional foul committed in the defending goal circle results in a penalty stroke to the other team (see penalty strokes).

Penalty strokes
Penalty strokes are awarded when a:
- defending player commits an intentional foul within the goal area
- goal would probably have been scored if a defender had not unintentionally committed a foul inside the circle.

Penalty strokes are taken from the penalty spot with only the goalkeeper defending the shot.

Other
Each team has seven players consisting of six outfield players and a goalkeeper. The game consists of two halves lasting 10 minutes each. Teams change ends at half-time.

Rules for hockey

Equipment
- One ball (between 156 g and 163 g in weight and between 22.4 cm and 23.5 cm in circumference).
- Two goals (3.65 m wide × 2.13 m high).
- One stick for each player (see page 20 for how to make equipment).
- Goalkeepers should wear some protective clothing, for example extra padding/material, particularly on the elbows and knees, solid footwear, gloves and some sort of protective head and face gear.
- A pitch with the correct measurements and markings.

Aim of the game
The aim is to score goals, using the hockey stick to hit the ball into the opponent's goal.

Starting the game
The game begins with one team passing the ball back from the centre spot. Teams must be in their own half of the field during the pass-back.

Pitch measurements and markings for hockey

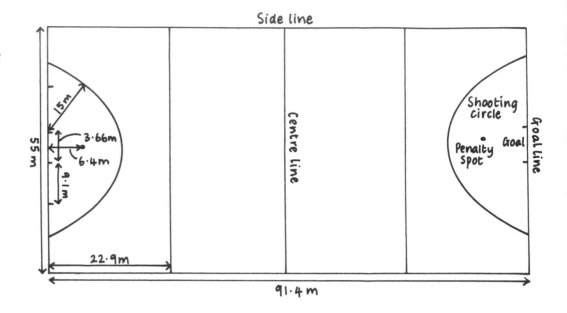

Side line

15 m

55 m

3.66 m

6.4 m

9.1 m

22.9 m

Centre line

Shooting circle

Penalty spot

Goal

Goal line

91.4 m

Scoring

A goal is scored when a player successfully hits the ball into the goal, from within the goal circle. The winner is the team with the most goals at the end of the match.

When a goal is scored, the game restarts with a pass-back to the team that conceded the goal.

When the ball goes out-of-bounds

The game stops when the ball goes out-of-bounds and restarts with one of the following:

► A **side line pass** is taken when the ball goes out along the side line. The team who last touched the ball loses possession and the ball is hit in by the other team from behind the line where the ball went out of play.

► A **goal hit** is taken when a team causes the ball to cross the goal line it is attacking. The defending team takes a free hit taken level with the top of the circle and opposite where the ball crossed the goal line.

► A **long corner** is taken when a team, from within 22.9 m of the goal line, unintentionally causes the ball to cross its own goal line. The other team takes a free hit from the corner. If the ball was last touched more than 22.9 m from the goal line, the other team take a free hit 15 m from the goal line, opposite where the ball went out of play.

► A **penalty corner** is taken when a team intentionally causes the ball to cross its own goal line. The other team takes a penalty corner from the corner of the pitch nearest to where the ball went out of play.

When a penalty corner is taken, no players may be in the goal circle except for the defending goalkeeper. Up to five defending players may stand on the goal line and move into the goal circle when the ball is played.

Fouls

A foul is called when a player:

► kicks, pushes, obstructs or trips an opposing player
► touches the ball with any part of the body or anything other than the flat side of the stick (except for the goalkeeper who may use the hands and feet to control the ball)
► plays the ball in a dangerous way.

When a foul is committed unintentionally, outside the goal circle, the other team is awarded a free hit from where the foul took place. An intentional foul committed within 22.9 m of the defending goal line, but outside of the goal circle, results in a penalty corner to the other team. An unintentional foul committed inside the defending circle results in a penalty corner to the other team. An intentional foul committed within the defending goal circle results in a penalty stroke to the other team (see penalty strokes below).

Penalty strokes

Penalty strokes are awarded when a:

► defending player commits an intentional foul within the goal area
► goal would probably have been scored if a defender had not unintentionally committed a foul inside the circle.

Penalty strokes are taken from the penalty spot with only the goalkeeper defending the shot.

Other

Each team has 11 players consisting of 10 outfield players and a goalkeeper. The game consists of two halves lasting 35 minutes each. Teams change ends at half-time.

Try-scoring games

In try-scoring games, a try is scored by placing the ball over the line your opponents are defending. Skills include running, passing and kicking.

Stage 1 *Running and chasing*

Objectives

To help students learn basic attacking skills, by running away from defenders, and basic defending skills, by chasing and catching attackers.

Equipment

► Markers to indicate a centre line.
► A line at each end of the playing area.

Safety
▶ Make sure pairs are well spaced.

Activity
▶ In pairs, players are numbered 1 or 2 and stand back-to-back in the middle of the playing area.
▶ If the teacher calls '1', the number 1s have to run to their line as fast as possible, while the number 2s chase and try to tag them (touch the person they are chasing to indicate they have caught them) before they reach it. If the teacher calls '2', the number 2s run to their line as fast as possible, while the number 1s chase and try to tag them before they reach it.
▶ Players count the number of times they tag their partner.

To make the activity easier for the chasers:
▶ increase the distance so they have more time to catch up.

To make the activity more difficult for the chasers:
▶ decrease the distance so they have less time to catch up
▶ let the runners go before the chasers, for example call '1' then '2'.

Teaching points

Ask the students
▶ **How can you reach the line quicker?**
Anticipate the call from the teacher.
React and move immediately.
Run as fast as possible at all times; do not be tempted to slow down even if you think you will not be caught before the line.

▶ **How can you tag your partner quicker?**
Anticipate the call from the teacher.
React immediately and start running as you are turning to face your partner.
Run as fast as you can until your partner has gone over the line; do not be tempted to give up if you think you will not catch your partner.

Stage 2 *Running and dodging*

Objectives
To help students improve their attacking skills by running past defenders, and their defending skills by catching the attackers as they try to pass.

Equipment
▶ Markers for playing area.
▶ One ball per group.

Safety
▶ Groups must remain in their own playing area.

Activity
▶ In groups of three, Player 1 runs inside the playing area with the ball to the other side, trying not to be tagged by Player 2. Player 2 tries to tag Player 1 but cannot chase once Player 1 has passed.

- ► Player 1 passes the ball to Player 3, who repeats the role of Player 1 but runs in the opposite direction.
- ► Players 1 and 3 count the number of successful dodges and Player 2 counts number of tags.
- ► Players change roles on the teacher's call.

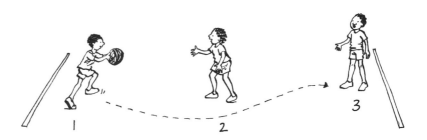

To make the activity easier for the runners:
- ► Player 2 can only take one step in any direction.

To make the activity more difficult for the runners:
- ► reduce the width of the playing area.

Teaching points

Ask the runners
- ► **How can you get to the other side without being tagged?**
  Commit Player 2 to moving one way so there is space to run.
  Use quick dodging movements and run as fast as possible.

Ask the tacklers
- ► **How can you prevent the runners from passing?**
  Anticipate the movements of the runners and mark them closely.
  Be prepared to change direction quickly.

Stage 3 *Running and passing*

Objectives
To help students learn how to pass and catch the ball on the run.

Equipment
- ► Large areas of playing space.
- ► One ball per group of three (preferably a rugby ball or equivalent). A rugby ball is oval shaped, measuring approximately 28 cm in length and 59 cm in width or circumference.

Safety
- ► Keep groups well spaced.

Activity
- ► In teams of three, players start in a diagonal line and start running forwards.
- ► Player 1 starts by passing backwards to Player 2 and running

behind the other players to the end of the line. Player 2 then passes to Player 3 and runs to the end of the line.

▶ Players continue this exercise until they run out of space and then repeat the exercise running and passing in the opposite direction.

▶ Teams lose a 'life' if they drop the ball and the winning team is the one with the least number of lost 'lives'.

To make the activity easier:
▶ run slowly or walk until passes are accurate
▶ players stay close together.

To make the activity more difficult:
▶ run faster and throw quicker
▶ players move further apart.

Teaching points

Ask the students

▶ **How do you make your passes accurate?**
Hold the ball with both hands: fingers spread and thumbs on the upper part of the ball. To throw the ball, twist your hips to bring your shoulders square to the receiver while running; take the ball back at hip level; bring your arms through quickly and strongly as you release the ball.
Throw the ball just in front of the receiver and between the waist and lower chest.

▶ **What must you remember when receiving the ball?**
Stay behind the person with the ball.
Put your hands out to receive the ball.

Stage 4 *Running, passing and try-scoring*

Objectives
To help students combine skills of attacking and scoring tries, and to encourage them to challenge other try-scorers.

Equipment
▶ Markers for playing area, including start and scoring line.
▶ One ball per group of three.

Safety
▶ Groups must remain in their own playing area.

Activity
▶ In groups of three, players start in a diagonal line.
▶ Player 1 passes to Player 2, who then passes to Player 3.
  ▶ Player 3 catches the ball, runs immediately to the end line and puts the ball on the ground with one or both hands without being caught. This is called a try.
  ▶ Players 1 and 2 try to tag Player 3 using both hands, before the ball touches the ground. They are not allowed to start chasing until Player 3 has the ball.
  ▶ Players rotate positions after each scoring attempt and count the number of times they score a try without being tagged.

To make the activity easier for the try-scorers:
▶ Players 1 and 2 do not chase Player 3.

To make the activity more difficult for try-scorers:
▶ make the scoring line further away so Players 1 and 2 have more time to catch Player 3.

Teaching points

See also page 76 for Teaching points for Stage 1.

Ask the students
▶ **How do you score a try?**
  Run for the line as fast as possible, immediately you have the ball.

Anticipate defenders' moves so you can dodge them.
Make sure the ball touches the ground over the line and with one or both hands touching.

Stage 5 *4 versus 2*

Objectives
To encourage attackers to work as a team and dodge the defenders to score tries, and to encourage defenders to prevent the attackers from scoring.

Equipment
▶ Markers for playing area.
▶ One ball per group.

Safety
▶ Players must not contact unless tagging.
▶ Groups must remain in their own playing area.

Activity
▶ Four attackers versus two defenders, with the attackers starting with the ball on their goal line and the defenders standing several metres in front of the attackers.

- The attackers can pass up and down their line and can attempt to score tries (see Stage 4) over the defender's goal line.
- The defenders can stop the attackers by tagging the player with the ball with both hands. If tagged, the player must pass the ball.
- Attackers score one point every time they score a try. If they pass the ball forwards, drop or kick it, they lose a point.
- Players change roles on the teacher's call and count the number of points scored.

To make the activity easier for the attackers:
- increase the size of the playing area.

To make the activity more difficult for the attackers:
- attackers must score a try within 10 passes and if they fail to do this, they lose a point.

Teaching points

Ask the attackers
- **How can you improve your score?**
  Let your team know where and when you want to receive the pass.
  Run to an open space but stay behind the person with the ball.

Ask the defenders
- **How can you stop the attackers from scoring?**
  Anticipate where the passes are going so you can intercept or chase the person with the ball.

Rules for touch rugby

Equipment
- One rugby ball. Use an oval-shaped ball measuring approximately 28 cm in length and 59 cm in width circumference. However, smaller balls may be used according to the ages and sizes of the students.
- A large area of flat ground.
- A pitch with the correct measurements and markings.

Aim of the game
The aim is to carry the ball over the opponent's goal line and place it on the ground, and to stop the opponents from carrying the ball over the goal line you are defending.

Starting the game
The game begins with one player passing the ball back to a player of their own team from the centre of the pitch. Teams must be in

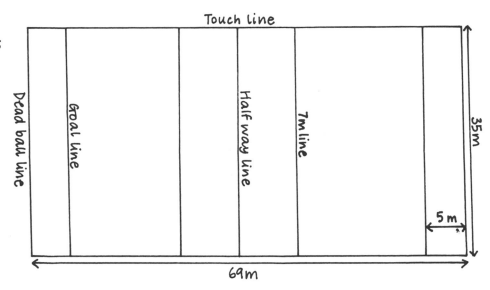

Pitch measurements and markings for touch rugby

their own halves during the pass back, and the opposing team must be at least 7 m from the half way line.

Scoring

A try is scored every time a team successfully places the ball on the ground over the opponent's goal line. The hand(s) must be on the ball as it contacts the ground. Five points are awarded for each try scored. The winner is the team with more points at the end of the match.

When the ball goes out-of-bounds

The game stops when the ball goes out-of-bounds along the side line. The team who last touched the ball loses possession. The other team pass the ball in from behind the side line where the ball went out of play.

Fouls

A foul is called when a player:
▶ passes or knocks the ball forwards; all passes must go sideways or backwards
▶ passes the ball within three strides of being touched (tackled) by an opposing player
▶ hands-off or fends-off an opposing player
▶ kicks the ball.

If a foul is committed, a free pass is awarded to the other team from where the foul took place.

Other

A game of touch rugby consists of two halves of equal length in time. Teams have equal numbers of between 9 and 12 players. Teams change ends at half-time.

Rules for rugby

Equipment
► One rugby ball. Preferably use an oval-shaped ball measuring approximately 28 cm in length and 59 cm in width circumference.
► A large area of flat ground.
► Two H-shaped goals.
► A pitch with the correct measurements and markings.

Aim of the game
The aim is to score more points than the opposing team by carrying the ball over the opponent's goal line and placing it on the ground or by kicking it between the posts above the cross-bar of the goal. The aim is also to stop the opponents from scoring points in this way.

Volunteers and colleagues recommend that students should always play touch rugby on playing surfaces that are hard.

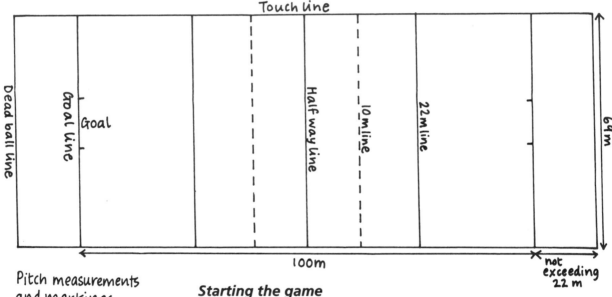

Pitch measurements and markings for rugby

Starting the game
The game begins with one team kicking the ball from the centre spot into the attacking half. This is called the kick-off. Teams must be in their own half during the kick-off and the opposing team must be behind the 10 m line.

Scoring
Points are scored in the following ways.
► A **try** is scored when a team successfully places the ball on the ground over the opponent's goal line. The hand(s), arm(s) or upper body must be in contact with the ball as it contacts the ground. Five points are awarded for a try.
► A **conversion** is scored when a team successfully kicks the ball between the goalposts above the cross-bar, after scoring a try. It is taken in line with where the try was scored and as far back as you wish. Two points are awarded for a conversion.
► A **penalty kick** is scored when a team successfully kicks the ball

between the goalposts above the cross-bar from a penalty. Three points are awarded for a penalty kick.

▶ A **drop goal** is scored when a team successfully kicks the ball between the goalposts above the cross-bar in open play. Three points are awarded for a drop goal.

The winner is the team with more points at the end of the match.

Players
Teams play with 15 players, of which eight are forwards and seven are backs. The positions of the forwards are hooker, loose-head prop, tight-head prop, left flanker, right flanker, left lock, right lock and number 8. The positions of the backs are full back, wingers, centres, scrum-half and fly-half.

When the ball goes out-of-bounds
The game stops when the ball goes out-of-bounds along the touch line. Play restarts with a line-out. Each team forms a line of at least two players, at a right angle to the touch line, opposite where the ball went out of play. The team who last touched the ball loses possession and the other team throws the ball in between the two lines of players, except where the ball is kicked out from a penalty, when the team kicking the ball retains possession.

Scrummage
A scrummage is taken when there is a stoppage in play, from where the stoppage occurred. The forward players from each team form the scrummage. Teams gather facing each other. The scrum-half from the team who was attacking prior to the stoppage puts the ball on the ground between the two teams, on the left-hand side. The hooker (the player at the front in the middle of the scrum) attempts to knock the ball backwards with the feet. When the ball emerges at the back of the scrum, play continues.

Fouls
A foul is called when a player:
▶ obstructs a player running for the ball
▶ strikes, kicks, stands on or trips with the foot an opposing player
▶ is in an offside position (see Glossary)
▶ passes or intentionally knocks the ball forwards; all passes must go backwards or sideways.

If a foul is committed, a free kick or penalty kick is awarded to the other team from where the foul took place. The team taking the kick has the option of taking a scrummage instead and puts in the ball (see scrummage above).

Other
A game of rugby consists of two halves of 40 minutes. Teams change ends at half-time.

Session plan

Date 3.6.98
Venue Sunny School
Time 2 p.m.
Duration 45 minutes
Group Boys and girls,
8/9 years
Number in group 40

Objectives
To help reinforce throwing and catching skills, to help students learn basic attacking skills of rugby by running away from defenders, and basic defending skills by chasing and catching attackers.

Equipment
▶ Markers to indicate a centre line.
▶ A line at each end of the playing area.

Organisation
Warm-up/introduction (5 minutes):
▶ tag – whoever gets caught becomes the new chaser
▶ drawing circles (see page 24, warm-up activities for young children)

Main content (30 minutes):
▶ 10 minutes, recap Activity 2, Stage 2 (see page 46)
▶ 10 minutes, recap Activity 4, Stage 2 (see page 46)
▶ 10 minutes, running and chasing (see page 89, try-scoring games)

Teaching points

Ask the students
▶ **How can you reach the line quicker?**
  Anticipate the call from the teacher.
  React and move immediately.
  Run as fast as possible at all times.
▶ **How can you tag your partner quicker?**
  Anticipate the call from the teacher.
  React immediately and start running as you turn to face your partner.
  Run as fast as you can until your partner has gone over the line.

▶ **How can you make it easier for the chasers?**
  Increase the distance so they have more time to catch up.
▶ **How can you make it harder for the chasers?**
  Decrease the distance so they have less time to catch up.
  Let the runners go before the chasers (for example call '1' then '2').

Cool down (5 minutes):
▶ gentle jogging turning into walking around area
▶ draw circles activity (see page 24).

Collect all equipment

Recap (5 minutes)

Summarise the main teaching points. Ask the students:
▶ How many times out of 10 did you catch the ball?
▶ Think of two reasons why you did better sometimes than at other times.

Safety
▶ Make sure pairs are well spaced.
▶ Injuries – none.

7

Net games

By the end of this chapter, you will know how to teach net games. Net games share many similar skills and the activities in this chapter develop and practise these skills. The chapter then lists the rules for mini and full games of volleyball.

Introduction

Net games can be played individually or with a partner (for example 1 versus 1 or 2 versus 2 in tennis) and can be team games (for example volleyball). The term net can be used to describe any type of court division (see Chapter 2 for ideas on how to improvise a net). The games are played on a court, which determines the boundary of where the ball may land, and involve skills such as hitting, running and jumping. The aim is to make the ball land in your opponent's side of the court one more time than they can make it land in yours. The scoring systems differ according to the game. Learning the basic skills is important, but these games are also tactical and elements such as attack and defence need to be introduced.

Do not be tempted to introduce students to the full games of the different sports before you have worked through mini games. This is because students have more opportunity in mini games to practise their skills because there are generally less people involved in a smaller playing area. As a result they are far more likely to enjoy the games and improve their skills.

Net games can be divided into two main sections:
► individual net games, which include tennis, table tennis and badminton
► team net games, which include volleyball.

Unfortunately, individual net games require much equipment (for example table tennis tables, bats and balls, tennis courts, rackets and balls, shuttlecocks) and can only occupy a few students at a time (for example 1 versus 1 or 2 versus 2) compared to team net games. As it is unlikely for teachers to have access to the necessary equipment for these games and have only a small number of students in their classes, this chapter concentrates on team net games only.

Students need to learn some general skills before they can play more specific games related to volleyball. These will then prepare them for learning and playing the mini and full versions of volleyball, the rules of which are fully explained. The metric measurements for the pitch and equipment are the official ones stipulated in the rules for each sport. If space and equipment are limited, you should feel free to improvise and make the best of what is available.

Team net games

In team net games, such as volleyball, the ball is not allowed to bounce. Hands are used to hit or pass the ball and more than two players can make up a team. There are six on a team for volleyball. Players may pass the ball between them before sending it over the net (up to three touches are allowed in volleyball).

Stage 1 *Volley throws*

Objectives
To help students learn how to pass the ball to each other if the ball is above head height.

Pre-game exercise
▶ In pairs, the ball is played above head height (volleyed) to each other and the number of consecutive passes counted.

Equipment
▶ One ball per court.

Safety
▶ Tell students to move quickly out of the way after their turn.
▶ Make sure students stand well back from the person who is at the front.

Activity
▶ In teams of approximately four, Player 1 volleys the ball to Player 1 of the opposite team and then runs to the back of the line.
▶ Player 2 volleys the ball to Player 2 of the opposite team and then runs to the back of the line, and so on.
▶ Teams try to keep the ball in play. If they fail to do this, the other team scores a point.
▶ The winning team is the first team to score 10 points.

To make the activity easier:
▶ make the court area smaller
▶ lower the net, or use no net.

To make the activity more difficult:
▶ tell players to make use of the full court, to vary the position of their volleys
▶ make players clap their hands before they return the ball; this gives them less time.

Teaching points

Ask the students

▶ **What position should you be in when you volley?**

Move so you are underneath the ball as it descends, but keep the ball in sight, slightly in front of the body, and bend your knees slightly.

Put your arms above your head and spread your fingers.

Make contact with the ball at forehead height.

Volley

▶ **How should you contact the ball?**

Push the ball upwards with your hands. Follow through with your fingers and arms.

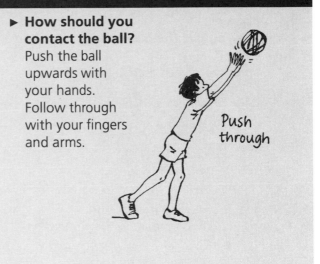

Push through

Stage 2 *Serving, digging and volleying*

Objectives

To help students learn how to start the game of volleyball, how to play the ball below head height (dig) and how to volley.

Equipment

▶ Half a court (or restricted area).
▶ One ball per pair.

Safety

▶ Keep students well spaced.
▶ Tell students not to collect balls from outside their area unless they are sure it is safe.

Activity

▶ 1 versus 1 per half court (or restricted area), Player 1 serves to Player 2.
▶ Player 2 digs the return back to Player 1 and players rally until the ball is dead, using either a volley or a dig.

To make the activity easier:

▶ practise serves only and digs only – Player 1 serves, Player 2 catches; Player 1 throws, Player 2 digs
▶ lower the net
▶ stand close together.

To make the activity more difficult:

▶ move further back
▶ make your opponent move and make points competitive, for example, the first to 10 points wins.

Teaching points

Ask the servers

▶ **How do you get the ball over the net and into court?**

Make a fist with your dominant hand.

Swing your arm from low to high.
Push forward and upward with your legs as you hit the ball.

Ask the diggers

▶ **What position should you be in when you dig?**

Put one foot in front of the other and move into position so your body is in line with the ball.

Bend your knees.
Lay the fingers of one hand across the palm of the other, keep your thumbs together and keep your arms firm and out in front.

▶ **How should you contact the ball?**

Make contact with the ball on the flat area when both hands are together.
Make your legs do the work – push with the legs as you make contact with the ball.
Keep your arms firmly locked on contact.

Stage 3 *Sets and strikes*

Objectives

To help students learn and practise the role of the setter (volleying the ball above head height and positioning it for a team mate to strike the ball) and the striker (attacking the ball with an overarm shot that aims to hit the ground on the opposite side of the net) in volleyball.

Equipment

▶ One volleyball and half a court (or restricted area) per group.

Safety

▶ Make sure players stay in their own area – do not let them collect balls from outside their area unless they know it is safe.

Activity

▶ In groups of three, Players 1 and 2 are on the same side of the net and Player 3 is on the other.
▶ Player 1 (the setter) throws the ball to Player 2 (the striker), who strikes the ball over the net to Player 3.
▶ Player 3 catches or collects the ball and throws it back to Player 1.
▶ Players repeat this five times and then change roles.

To involve more players, you can have more students line up behind Player 2. Players take turns to strike the ball and then change roles with Players 1 and 3 so that they can also practise striking the ball.

To make the activity easier:
▶ lower the net.

To make the activity more difficult:
▶ Player 1 releases the ball and volleys the ball instead of throwing it (sets the ball). Player 3 tries to retrieve the strike by digging back to Player 1, who immediately sets again for Player 2; players try to keep the ball moving.

Teaching points

Ask the setters
▶ **Where should you position the ball for the strikers?**
Position the ball above the head of the strikers and slightly in front of them so they can move forwards onto the ball.
Set/throw the ball high enough for the strikers to jump up and hit at maximum height.

Ask the strikers
▶ **How should you contact the ball?**
Strike the ball at maximum height, and use your legs to push upwards.
Strike the ball firmly with your dominant hand, aiming for the ground on the other side of the net.

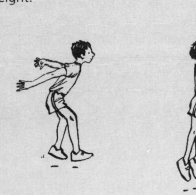

Stage 4 *Working in 4s*

Objectives
To help students learn when and how to serve, dig, set and strike.

Equipment
▶ One volleyball and half a court (or restricted area) per group.

Safety
▶ Make sure players stay in their own area, do not let them collect balls from outside their area unless it is safe.

Activity

- ▶ In groups of four, Players 2, 3 and 4 are on one side of the net and Player 1 is on the other.
- ▶ Player 1 (the server) throws the ball underarm to Player 2 (the digger), who catches it and throws it to Player 3 (the setter).
- ▶ Player 3 catches the ball and throws to Player 4 (the striker), who strikes the ball.
- ▶ Player 1 catches or collects the ball.
- ▶ Players repeat this five times and then change roles.

To make the activity easier:
- ▶ lower the net.

To make the activity more difficult:
- ▶ Player 1 serves instead of throws, Player 2 digs instead of catches, and Player 3 sets instead of catches; the players try to keep the ball moving between players.

Teaching points

Ask the setter
- ▶ **Where should you position the ball for the striker?**
  Position the ball above the head of the striker and slightly in front of them so they can move forwards onto the ball.
  Set/throw the ball high enough for the striker to jump up and hit at maximum height.

Ask the striker
- ▶ **How should you contact the ball?**
  Strike the ball at maximum height, using your legs to push up.
  Strike firmly with your dominant hand, aiming for the ground on the other side of the net.

Ask the diggers
- ▶ **How do you control the dig?**
  React and move quickly once you know where the serve is going.
  Direct the ball to where the setter wants it.

Ask the servers
- ▶ **How do you get the ball over the net and into court?**
  Make a fist with your dominant hand.
  Swing your arm from low to high.
  Push forward and upward with your legs as you hit the ball.

Stage 5 *3 versus 3 volleyball*

Objectives
To help students learn how to use their skills in a game situation.

Equipment
- ▶ One volleyball and half a court (or restricted area) per group.

Safety
- ▶ Make sure students stay in their own area – do not let them collect balls from outside their area unless it is safe.

Activity

- ► 3 versus 3 in a half court (or restricted area).
- ► One team starts serving and the serve must go directly over the net and into the court.
- ► After the serve, the ball may be touched up to three times on one side of the net before it has to reach the other side.
- ► The team who wins the point, wins the serve; teams only score when they are serving.
- ► Players continue to serve as long as their team wins the point, and then players take turns to serve and change positions on the court. Each player moves one place clockwise as a new player serves; this encourages players to learn the skills and tactics of the different positions on the court.

To make the activity easier:
- ► lower the net
- ► to start the rally, throw the ball instead of serving
- ► use a small playing area.

To make the activity more difficult:
- ► increase the playing area.

Volunteers and colleagues recommend that to help students have fun and keep their interest in the game, any number of touches and bounces is allowed. This encourages the ball to keep moving. The point is lost when the ball is dead.

Teaching points

Ask the players
- ► **What do you do if the ball goes down the middle of the court?**

Communicate with your team about who is taking the ball and how/where they should send it.
Call firmly and use simple words, for example, mine, set, over.

Ask the players
- ► **How can you make sure you develop good technique and teamwork?**

Avoid being tempted to use one hand only, instead of volleying and digging.
Avoid hitting the ball straight back to the opposition; instead you should pass to other players on your team (teamwork) to build the attack.

Rules for mini volleyball

Equipment
► One ball (soft and light).
► One net, approximately 2.1 m high (see page 21 for how to make equipment).
► A small area of flat ground with the correct court measurements and markings.

Court measurements and markings for mini volleyball

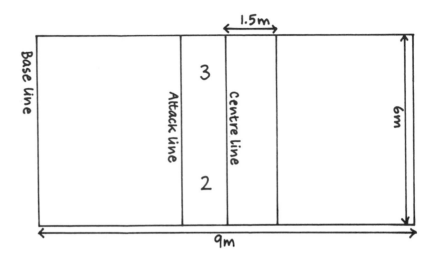

Aim of the game
The aim of mini volleyball is to use the hands to:
► make the ball touch the opponent's playing area
► play the ball in such a way that the opponents cannot return it.

Starting the game
One team starts with the ball. Play begins with the player in position 1 on the starting team serving the ball. Players can serve from anywhere along the baseline.

Scoring
When a team faults, the opposing team wins the rally. If the opposing team was:
► serving, it scores one point and continues to serve
► receiving, it gains the right to serve, but does not score a point.

A set is won by the first team to score 15 points, by two clear points. In the event of a 16–16 tie, the team who scores the next point wins the set. The team who wins two sets wins the match.

After each set, teams change ends. In the third set, the teams also change ends when a team reaches eight points.

Faults
A fault is called when a:
► player fails to serve the ball over the net into the opponent's court

- team fails to return the ball into the opponent's side of the court within a maximum of three touches of the ball
- player touches the ball twice in succession in a point
- player touches the net
- player is not in the correct rotational order.

Players' positions
Each team consists of three players who rotate around three playing positions. When a team gains service, it rotates around one position so that the player in position 2 moves to position 1 and becomes the server. The same player continues to serve until the team loses the serve.

Rules for volleyball

Equipment
- One volleyball (65–67 cm in circumference, 260–280 g in weight).
- One net (1 m in depth and 9.5 m long, with a height of 2.43 m for boys and 2.24 m for girls), supported by two posts (2.55 m high and fixed to the ground at a distance of 0.5 m–1 m from each side line (see page 21 for how to make equipment).
- A small area of flat ground with the correct court measurements and markings.

Court measurements and markings for volleyball

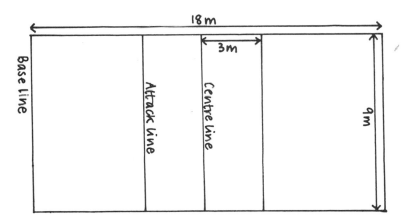

Aim of the game
The aim of volleyball is to use the hands to:
- make the ball touch the opponent's playing area
- play the ball in such a way that the opponents cannot return it.

Starting the game
One team starts with the ball. Play begins with the player in position 1 on the starting team serving the ball. Players can serve from anywhere along the baseline.

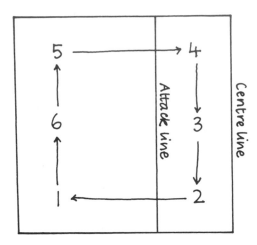

Player positions and rotations for volleyball

Scoring

When a team faults, the opposing team wins the rally. If the opposing team was:

► serving, it scores one point and continues to serve
► receiving, it gains the right to serve, but does not score a point.

A set is won by the first team to score 15 points, by two clear points. In the event of a 16–16 tie, the team who scores the next point wins the set. The team who wins three sets wins the match. In the event of a 2–2 tie, the fifth set is played with a point being awarded after every fault, regardless of server.

After each set, teams change ends. In a deciding set, teams change ends when a team reaches eight points.

Faults

A fault is called when a:

► player fails to serve the ball over the net into the opponent's court
► team fails to return the ball into the opponent's side of the court with a maximum of three touches of the ball
► player touches the ball twice in succession before returning it over the net
► player touches the net
► player is out of the correct rotational order.

Players' positions

Each team consists of six players who rotate around six playing positions. Every player will play in all six positions. When a team gains service, it rotates around one position so that the player in position 2 moves to position 1 and becomes the server. The same player continues to serve until the team loses the serve.

Substitutions

Up to six substitutions may be made per team per set and one or more players may be substituted at the same time. A player of the starting line-up may leave the court and re-enter only once in a set, and must return to their starting position. A substitute player may enter the court only once per set.

Session plan

<u>Date</u> 3.7.98
<u>Venue</u> Sunny School
<u>Time</u> 2 p.m.
<u>Duration</u> 45 minutes
<u>Group</u> Boys and girls,
  8/9 years
<u>Number in group</u> 40

<u>Objectives</u>
For students to recap on basic throwing and catching skills and to help them learn how to pass the ball using volley throws.

<u>Equipment</u>
▶ Playing area
▶ One ball (any type) per pair for the first two activities
▶ One volleyball
▶ Net (optional)
▶ Playing area per pair/group of four/two teams for the main activities

<u>Organisation</u>
Warm-up/introduction (5 minutes):
▶ running game in pairs, take turns to run to the net and back
▶ drawing circles (see page 24, warm-up activities for young children)
▶ running game in pairs, run to the net, draw a circle (as above), and then run back to the base.

Main content (30 minutes)
Team net games
▶ 5 minutes – Stage 3, Activity 1 (see page 102)
▶ 5 minutes – Stage 2, Activity 1 (see pages 101–102)
▶ 10 minutes – Stage 1, pre-game exercise (see page 100).
▶ 10 minutes – Stage 1, volley throws (see page 100).

If there are not enough balls for the pre-game exercise, use one ball per group of four: students can pass in the direction of a square or a circle.

Teaching points

Ask the students
▶ **What position should you be in when you volley?**
Move so you are underneath the ball as it descends, but keep the ball in sight, slightly in front of the body, and bend your knees slightly.
Put your arms above your head and spread your fingers.
Make contact with the ball at forehead height.

Volley

▶ **How should you contact the ball?**
Push the ball upwards with your hands.
Follow through with your fingers and arms.

Push through

Cool down (5 minutes):
▶ walking around playing area in a big circle and drawing circles (see page 24) when instructed

Collect all equipment

Recap (5 minutes)

Summarise the main teaching points. Ask the students:
▶ What was your longest rally with your partner (or group of four) in the preliminary exercises?
▶ If the rally broke down, or you lost a point in the team game, what was the reason?
▶ What must you remember next time?

Safety
▶ Tell students to move quickly out of the way after their turn.
▶ Make sure students stand well back from the person who is at the front.
▶ Injuries – none.

8

Batting and fielding games

By the end of this chapter, you should be able to teach batting and fielding games. The chapter outlines many skills and practices and then lists the rules for mini and full games of cricket, rounders and softball.

Volunteers and colleagues recommend this game because it involves lots of students and lots of activity.

Introduction

Batting and fielding games are played in teams, where one team bats while the other one fields. These games involve skills such as hitting, running, throwing and catching. Individual skills and team tactics are important in teaching these games. The following pages give you some examples of more specific activities you can introduce to students and how they can progress towards playing a full game.

Do not be tempted to introduce students to the full games of the different sports before you have worked through the mini games. Students have more opportunity in mini games to practise their skills because there are generally less people involved in a smaller playing area. As a result they are far more likely to enjoy the games and improve their skills.

This chapter is divided into three main sections:
▶ **batting games** which develop mainly batting and running skills
▶ **fielding games** which develop mainly catching and throwing skills
▶ **combining batting and fielding games** for example teeball, cricket, rounders and softball.

The first two sections develop the skills that students need to play batting and fielding games. The last section on the specific games covers the rules for both the mini and full versions of each game.

The metric measurements given for the pitch and equipment are the official ones required by the rules of each sport. If space and equipment are limited, you should feel free to improvise and to make the best use of whatever is available.

Batting games

Batting games involve striking the ball with a bat and running to score runs or points. They help students to develop batting skills, including the direction and speed of the ball, and running skills, including quick turns. The games in this section combine running and batting skills.

Stage 1 *Running rounders*

Objectives
To help students learn the concept of rounders without the complication of hitting the ball, and to help them improve running, throwing and catching skills.

Equipment
► One ball per group.
► Four markers per group.

Safety
► Keep groups well spaced.

Activity
► In groups of 4 versus 4, each group places four markers in a square/circle as if for rounders.
► Team A positions each player at one of the markers/posts.
► Player 1 of Team B gets ready to run from first base and the rest of the players in Team B line up behind Player 1.
► On the command of 'go', Player 1 of Team A throws to Player 2 of Team A. At the same time, Player 1 of Team B tries to reach the first post before the ball.
► Player 2 of Team A immediately throws to the next player, and so on.
► Player 1 of Team B tries to reach the fourth post before the ball and then Player 2 of Team B repeats.
► When all players have had a turn, the teams change roles. The number of times players reach the fourth post before the ball is counted.

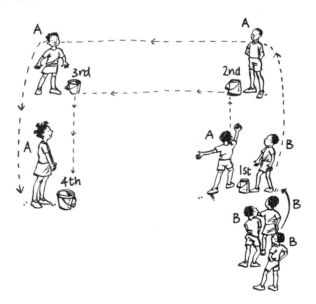

To make the activity easier for Team B:
► put four extra players in the fielding team, one between each post, so the ball has an extra stop between posts; this gives the runners more time.

To make the activity more difficult for Team B:
► make the runners circle each post, at posts 1, 2 and 3, before they run on to the next.

Teaching points

Ask the runners
▶ **How can you get to fourth post quicker?**
  Turn quickly at the posts.
  Stay close to the markers as you turn.

Stage 2 *Batting for cricket*

Objectives
To help students learn how to hit the ball in different directions and with control.

Equipment
▶ One bat per group.
▶ One ball per group.

Safety
▶ Keep groups well spaced.

Activity
▶ Put the students in groups of four with Player 2 facing the other three.
▶ Player 1 throws the ball underarm to Player 2.
▶ Player 2 lets the ball bounce and bats to Player 3, who catches the ball and throws it back to Player 2.
▶ Player 2 hits to each catcher in turn and players change places after each round.

To make the activity easier:
▶ players throw and hit non-competitively – that is, for accuracy and not to beat the other players.

To make the activity more difficult:
▶ players stand further apart
▶ players increase the speed of their throws and hits.

Teaching points

Ask the batters
▶ **How do you make good contact?**
  Grip and angle the bat.
  Keep your wrists firm on contact.
  Watch the ball closely and keep your head still on contact.

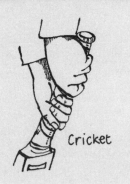

Cricket

Stage 3 *Batting for distance*

Objectives:
To encourage students to hit for length when they are batting, for softball and rounders.

Equipment
▶ One bat per group.
▶ One ball per group.
▶ Four markers per group.

Safety
▶ Keep groups well spaced.

Activity
▶ Put students in groups of up to 10 players, with each group making a square using four markers. The square should be made smaller for young children and beginners.
▶ Players take turns to bat, bowl, backstop and field.
▶ Bowlers throw the ball underarm (without it bouncing) to the batter, who does not run after hitting, but scores one point for hitting inside the square, two points for hitting beyond the square and three points for hitting into an outer boundary.
▶ Players change places after five bats.

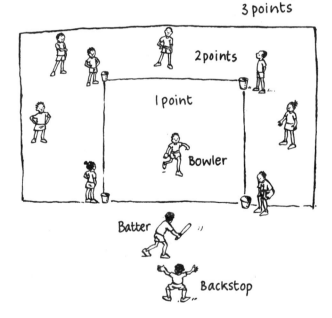

Please note that this game can also be played with cricket bats, but the bowlers should throw the ball so that it bounces before the batter hits.

To make the activity easier:
▶ make the square smaller
▶ the bowler throws non-competitively and with little pace so that the batter has more time to hit the ball.

To make the activity more difficult:
▶ make the square bigger
▶ the bowler varies the throws, for example, throwing more quickly or with more spin.

Teaching points

Ask the batters
▶ **How should you hold the bat?**
Use two hands for softball and one hand for rounders.

▶ **How do you develop good timing?**
Take the bat back as the ball is travelling towards you.
Swing the bat through quickly to hit the ball.
Follow through after you have hit the ball.

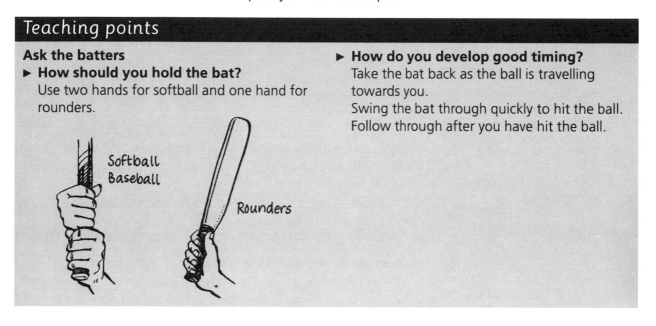

Softball
Baseball

Rounders

Stage 4 *One-post rounders*

Objectives
To help students make decisions about whether to run for a rounder and to give them the chance to practise their batting skills in a competitive situation.

Equipment
▶ Markers for batting base, bowling base and post.
▶ One bat per pitch.
▶ One ball per pitch.

Safety
▶ Make sure batters who are waiting to have their turn keep out of the way.

Activity
▶ In groups of 4 versus 4 or 5 versus 5, Player 1 bowls to Player 2. Player 2 bats, runs to the post and either stops there or returns to base before the ball, in which case a rounder is scored.
▶ If Player 2 stops at the post, the next batter receives the bowl. Player 2 cannot run back to base until the bowler has released the ball.
▶ Batters must run, whether or not they hit the ball, and the fielders must try to get the batters out by catching the hit before the bounce or getting the ball to either post before the batter.
▶ The batting team count the number of rounders and teams change roles on the teacher's call.
▶ The winning team is the one with the most rounders.

To make the activity easier for the batters:
▶ use bats with a larger hitting surface.

To make the activity more difficult for the batters:
▶ bowlers vary their throws, for example, they throw more quickly or with more spin.

Teaching points

Ask the batters
▶ **What must you remember when batting?**
Think carefully whether you have a good chance of scoring a rounder before you leave the post and run back to base.
Run immediately the ball has left the hands of the bowler if you are at a post, or immediately you have hit the ball if you are batting.
Hit the ball away from the fielders to avoid being caught out.
Keep your eyes on the ball and your head still.

Fielding games

Fielding games help students to develop throwing and catching skills. They encourage teamwork and communication between fielders.

Stage 1 *Bowling and wicket keeping*

Objectives
To help students learn how to bowl for accuracy and how to catch the oncoming ball if they are the wicket keeper for cricket.

Equipment
▶ Markers for the target area, wicket keeper and the line at which the ball must be delivered.

▶ One wicket per group.
▶ One ball per group.

Safety
▶ Keep groups well spaced.

Activity
▶ In groups of thrée, Player 1 bowls overarm, over or around the wicket, and directs the ball to bounce in the target area.
▶ Player 2 catches and returns the ball to Player 1.
▶ Player 3 counts the number of balls that bounce in the target area and the number of times the ball hits the wicket.

Target area

Wicket

▶ Player 1 delivers 12 balls, which is two overs, before players change positions. An over is six balls bowled from one wicket to the other.

To make the activity easier:
▶ play the game bowling from a stand still, with no run up
▶ increase the target area
▶ decrease the distance between the bowling line and the wicket.

To make the activity more difficult:
▶ decrease the target area
▶ increase the distance between the bowling line and the wicket.

Teaching points

Ask the students
▶ **How should you hold the ball when you throw?**
Hold the ball with your fingers and not the whole hand.
Support the ball underneath with the thumb.

▶ **How should you prepare to throw?**
Turn sideways at the bowling line, hold the ball close to chin, and put your weight on the back foot.
Extend the non-throwing arm and direct it towards the target.
Extend your throwing arm above your head, so you release the ball at the highest point.
Transfer your weight as you release the ball.

▶ **How should you follow through?**
Step forwards as you swing and follow through with the throwing arm.
Look at the wicket as you throw and keep your head still.
▶ **How do you prepare to stop the ball as wicket keeper?**
Keep your eyes on the ball and your head still.
Cup your hands together and out in front.
Bend your knees and rest your weight on the balls of your feet.

Stage 2 *Pitching, backstop and fielding*

Objectives
To help students learn and practise their batting and fielding skills in a competitive situation.

Equipment
► Markers for bowler, batter, backstop and post.
► One ball per group of six.
► One hoop per group of six.

Safety
► Keep runners out of the way unless it is their turn.
► Keep teams well spaced.

Activity
► Form groups of six, three runners versus three fielders.
► Player 1 (the pitcher) throws underarm to Player 3, aiming to get the ball through the hoop.
► Player 2 runs to the post as soon as the ball goes past, while Player 3 catches/stops the ball and immediately throws to Player 4.
► If the runners touch the post before Player 4 touches it with the ball, they are 'in'. If not, the fielding team score a point.
► The number of points scored in 5 minutes is counted and then teams change roles.

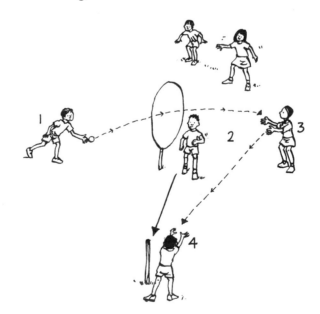

To make the activity easier:
► pitchers throw more slowly
► play the game without the runners: the pitcher throws to the backstop, the backstop throws to the fielder on the post, and the fielder throws to the bowler.

To make the activity more difficult:
► pitchers vary their throws, for example they throw more quickly or with more spin.

Ask the pitchers
▶ **How should you prepare to pitch?**
Face the batter with your weight on the back foot as the throwing arm is raised.
Step forwards (with the opposite leg to the throwing arm) as the arm swings downwards and forwards, and the ball is released.
Make the arm action slow at first, but then make it fast and snappy by using the wrist as the ball is released.

Ask the backstops
▶ **How do you prevent the ball from going past?**
Stand with your feet slightly apart, with your knees relaxed and eyes in line with the ball. Place both hands in front of your body.
▶ **How do you get the runner out?**
Throw the ball quickly and accurately to the fielder at the post, immediately you have caught or stopped the ball.

Ask the fielders:
▶ **How can you get the runner out?**
Anticipate the throw from the backstop so you can prepare for the catch.
Touch the post with the ball immediately after you have caught it.

Stage 3 *Non-stop rounders*

Objectives
To encourage students to practise their skills for rounders in a competitive situation.

Equipment
▶ One ball per group.
▶ One bat per group.
▶ Three markers per group.

Safety
▶ Keep groups well spaced.

Activity
▶ In groups of five, each group places a marker for the bowler, batter and post.

- Batters receive five underarm bowls (no bounce) and to score a run they have to run around the post and back before the ball is fielded and returned to the bowler.
- After every fifth ball the players move around one place anti-clockwise.
- The winner is the player with the most runs after a given number of batting turns. Batters always receive five balls; they are never out before this, even if they are caught out or they fail to get back to the starting post before the bowler receives the ball.

To make the activity easier for the fielders:
- place the marker for the post further away from the hitting point.

To make the activity more difficult for the fielders:
- place the marker for the post closer to the hitting point.

Teaching points

Ask the fielders
- **How do you prevent the batters from scoring?**
  As backstop, anticipate the throw from the bowler and return the ball immediately if the batter fails to hit it.
  As fielder, return the ball to the bowler as quickly as possible.

Stage 4 *Non-stop cricket*

Objectives
To encourage students to practise their skills for cricket in a competitive situation.

Equipment
- Markers for bowler and batters.
- One bat.
- One ball (see pages 19–20 for how to make equipment).
- One wicket.

Safety
- If two games are taking place at the same time, make sure they are well spaced from each other.
- Do not use hard balls.

Activity
- Organise a playing area and divide the players into two teams of equal numbers (5–10 players per team). One team is batting, the other is fielding.
- For the fielding team, choose a bowler and a backstop and spread out the remaining fielders.
- The bowlers bowl underarm and throw again, immediately after the fielders have returned the ball to them.
- Batters run to either mark and back after every bowl, aiming to

get back before the next bowl; they score one point every time they get back to base unless they hit their own wicket.

▶ The bowler hits the wicket or the fielders catch the ball from a hit; if they fail to score a point they are out and the next batter on the team has their turn.

▶ Teams change over when the batting team is all out.

▶ When both teams have batted, the winning team is the one with more points.

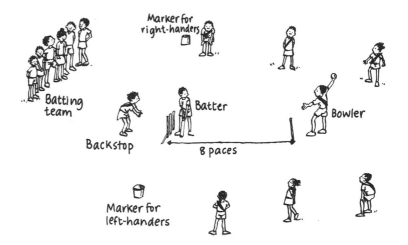

To make the activity easier for the batters:
▶ place the markers closer to the wicket.

To make the activity more difficult for the batters:
▶ place the markers further from the wicket.

Teaching points

Ask the fielders
▶ **How do you prevent the batters from scoring?**
As backstop, anticipate the throw from the bowler and return the ball immediately if the batter fails to hit it.
As fielder, return the ball to the bowler as quickly as possible.
As bowler, bowl immediately after receiving the ball and aim for the wickets.

Combining batting and fielding games

Games such as teeball, softball, rounders and cricket combine batting and fielding games.

Rules for teeball

Equipment
- One bat.
- One ball.
- Four markers.
- One tee. A tee is an object on which the ball can rest, so the game can be played without a pitcher.
- A large area of flat ground with the correct pitch measurements and markings.

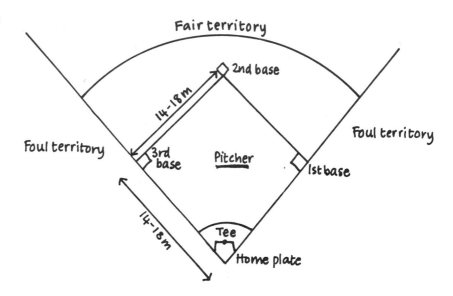

Pitch measurements and markings for teeball

Aim of the game
The aim of teeball is to score more runs than the opposing team by:
- scoring runs when batting
- preventing the opposing team from scoring runs when batting.

Starting the game
One team starts to bat, one team fields. The first batter attempts to hit the ball off the tee into fair territory. If the ball is hit into fair territory, the batter must run to first base, and further if possible. The remainder of the batting team then continues to bat in order.

Scoring
A run is scored when a batter succeeds in running round all of the bases and back to the home base without being run or caught out (see under Batters out).

Batting
The batter attempts to hit the ball from the home plate into the fair territory. If this is achieved, the batter must run to first base. A batter is out if three strikes are given. A strike is given if the batter:

- swings and misses the ball
- hits the tee and the ball falls off.

Only one batter may wait on each base. A batter waiting on a base does not have to run unless the batter immediately behind does so. If a batter is obstructed when attempting to reach a base the batter will be allowed to reach that base safely.

Batters out
A batter is out when:
- three strikes are given
- the base the batter is running to is tagged with the ball by a fielder, before the base is reached
- in attempting to reach the next base, the batter is tagged with the ball by a fielder
- a preceding batter is overtaken
- a fielder is obstructed when attempting to field the ball or get a batter out
- in attempting to avoid being tagged, the batter runs outside of the baseline.

When three batters are out, the innings is over and teams change so the fielding team becomes the batting team.

Other
Each team consists of nine players, although this may vary as long as teams are equal. Each team bats for seven innings. The winner is the team scoring the most runs at the end of all innings.

Rules for softball

Equipment
- One bat.
- One ball.
- Four markers.
- A large area of flat ground with the correct pitch measurements and markings.

Aim of the game
The aim of softball is to score more runs than the opposing team by:
- scoring runs when batting
- preventing the opponents from scoring runs when batting.

Starting the game
One team starts to bat and one team fields. The game starts with the pitcher pitching (bowling) to the first batter of the opposing team. If the batter hits the ball into fair territory the batter must run to first base, or may run further if possible. The remainder of the batting team continues to bat in order.

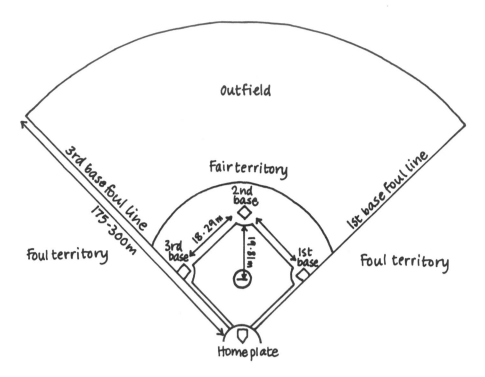

Pitch measurements and markings for softball

outfield

Fair territory

3rd base foul line

175–300m

1st base foul line

2nd base

3rd base

18.29m

19.81m

1st base

Foul territory

Foul territory

Home plate

Scoring

A run is scored when a batter succeeds in running round all of the bases and back to the home base without being run or caught out (see under Batters out).

Batting

The batter attempts to hit the ball from the home plate into the fair territory. If this is achieved, the batter must run to first base. A batter is out if three strikes are given. A strike is given if the batter:
- ▶ fails to hit a ball pitched in the strike zone, the area between the batter's shoulders and knees when in batting position
- ▶ hits the ball into foul territory – this does not apply if it is the third strike
- ▶ swings at the ball and misses.

Only one batter may wait on each base. A batter waiting on a base is not obliged to run unless the batter immediately behind does so. If a batter is obstructed when attempting to reach a base the batter will be allowed to reach that base safely.

Batters out

A batter is out when:
- ▶ three strikes are given
- ▶ the base is tagged with the ball by a fielder, before the batter touches it
- ▶ in attempting to reach the next base, the batter is tagged with the ball by a fielder
- ▶ a preceding batter is overtaken
- ▶ a fielder is obstructed when attempting to field the ball or get a batter out.

When three batters are out, the innings is over and teams change so the fielding team becomes the batting team.

Other

Each team consists of nine players. Each team bats for seven innings. The winner is the team scoring the most runs at the end of all the innings.

Rules for mini cricket

Equipment
- ► Two sets of stumps (see page 21 for how to make equipment).
- ► Two bats.
- ► One ball.
- ► Six fielding markers.
- ► A playing area of flat ground with the correct pitch markings.

Pitch measurements
and markings
for mini cricket

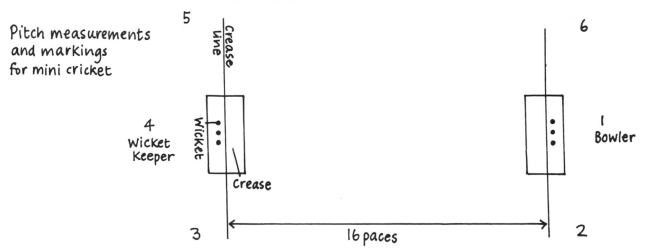

Aim of the game

The aim of mini cricket is to finish the match with a higher score of runs than the opposing team. This is achieved by scoring runs when batting, and deducting runs from the opposition by getting them out when fielding.

Starting the game

One team bats and one team fields. The batting team starts with a score of 100 runs. The first batting pair take their places in front of the wickets. The fielding team takes position on the field and the bowler proceeds to bowl to the first batter.

Scoring

A run is scored every time the batter runs from one wicket to the other when the ball is in play. The batters must run every time the ball is hit, or may choose to run if the ball is not hit. Four runs are awarded for a boundary. If playing indoors, the wall behind the bowler is the boundary. Three runs are deducted when a batter is 'out'.

Batting

The first batting pair bat for two overs. An over is six balls bowled from one wicket to the other. At the end of the two overs they are replaced by the second pair, who after two more overs are replaced by the third pair. When a batter is out, the batters change ends. However, the batters have unlimited lives and do not retire when out. At the end of each over, batters change ends.

Batters out
A batter is declared out when the:
► wicket is struck by the bowler bowling the ball
► wicket is struck by the batter defending the wicket
► ball is caught by a fielder after hitting the bat, before touching the ground
► ball is intercepted by the batter with any part of the body other than the bat or hand, where it would otherwise have hit the wicket
► wicket is touched with the ball while the batter is making a run, before the batter reaches the wicket
► wicket is touched with the ball by the wicket keeper of the fielding team when the batter is outside the crease.

Fielding
The fielding team rotates around six positions. The bowler bowls for one over. At the end of each over, the fielders all move round one place clockwise.

Other
Each team consists of six players. A game consists of one innings for each team. Teams change over after each innings. The team with the higher score wins.

Rules for cricket

Equipment
► Two sets of stumps (wickets).
► One ball.
► Two bats (see page 20 for how to make equipment).
► A large, flat playing area with the correct pitch measurements and markings.

Aim of the game
The aim of cricket is to score more runs than the opposing team. This is achieved by defending the wicket (the stumps being bowled at) when batting, by hitting the ball and making runs. When fielding, the aim is to stop the opposing team from making runs and to get all the players out.

Starting the game
One team bats and one team fields. The first two players of the batting team take their places in front of the wickets. The fielding players take their positions on the field and the bowler bowls to the first batter.

Pitch measurements and markings for cricket. (Boundary is not to scale.)

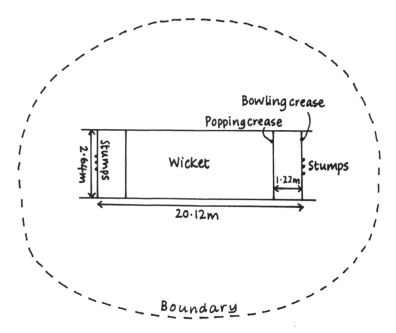

Scoring

A run is scored every time the first batsman runs from one wicket to the other while the ball is in play, without being run or caught out (see under Batters out). Runs are also awarded when the ball goes over the boundary line: four runs if the ball touches the ground first, and six if the ball is hit over the boundary without touching the ground. Penalty runs are awarded for a ball that is delivered too wide.

Batting

Teams bat in pairs. The bowler bowls to the batter at the far end, who attempts to hit the ball. The batter then has the option to run, whether or not the ball is hit. If the batter runs, the other batter must also run. The batters may stop running when they reach either wicket, and the bowler then bowls to the batter who is at the far end. If a boundary is scored, the batters need not run. If they have begun running, they return to the wickets they have left.

Batters out

A batter is declared out when the:
- ▶ wicket is struck by the bowler bowling the ball, even if the ball touches the bat or batter first
- ▶ wicket is struck by the batter attempting to defend the wicket
- ▶ ball is caught by a fielder after hitting the bat, before touching the ground
- ▶ ball is intercepted by the batter with any part of the body other than the bat or hand, where it would otherwise have hit the wicket
- ▶ wicket is touched with the ball while the batter is running from one wicket to another, before the batter reaches the crease line
- ▶ wicket is touched with the ball by the wicket keeper of the fielding team when the batter is outside the crease.

Fielding

The fielding team must have at least two bowlers. A bowler bowls the ball six times (one over). Overs are bowled from alternate ends and a bowler may not bowl two overs in succession. The rest of the fielding team attempt to field the ball as quickly as possible in order to get the batters out.

Other

Each team consists of 11 players. A game may consist of one or two innings. Teams change over after each innings. An innings is when all but one of the batters is out, or when a certain number of overs have been bowled; this may be determined by the teacher. The winner is the team with the greater number of runs at the end of the match. If the match is not played to a finish, it is regarded as a draw.

Rules for mini rounders

Equipment

- One bat (minimum).
- One ball.
- Four markers.
- A large area of flat ground with the correct pitch measurements and markings.

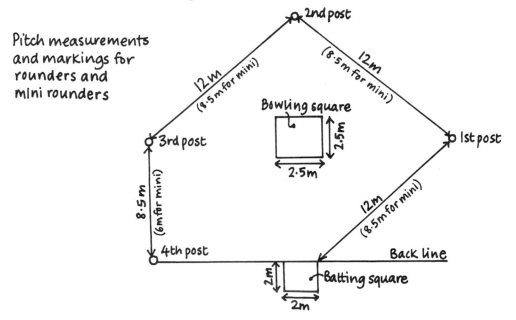

Pitch measurements and markings for rounders and mini rounders

Aim of the game

The aim is to score more rounders than the opposing team.

Starting the game

One team bats and one team fields. The game starts with the bowler bowling underarm to the first batsman of the opposing team. On receiving a good ball (see under No-ball), the batter must run to the first post, or may run on to other posts if possible. The remainder of the batting team continues to bat in order.

Scoring

Rounders are scored when a batter runs around the posts and touches the last one without being run or caught out (see under Batters out). If the fourth post is reached without stopping, three rounders are scored. If the fourth post is reached in a number of goes, only one rounder is scored.

One penalty rounder is given when the:
► batter reaches the fourth post without stopping, without having hit the ball
► bowler bowls two consecutive no-balls (see under No-balls) to the same batter
► batter is obstructed, for example from running from post to post.

Batting

A batter receives one good ball and must then run to first post. If the ball is hit into the backward area, the batter may not run beyond first post. The batter has the option to run on a no-ball, or receive another ball. Batters waiting on the posts may only run after the ball is bowled. A runner is not obliged to run unless the player immediately behind does so. Only one batter is allowed to wait on each post at any one time. A batter may not overtake another batter.

Batters out

A batter is declared out when:
► the ball is caught from the bat or a hand touching the bat
► a fielder touches the post the batter is running to, with the ball, before the batter has touched the post
► a fielder is obstructed or the direction of the ball is deliberately altered
► a batter in front is overtaken
► the bowler has the ball in the bowling square and the batter continues to run past the next post.

The innings is over when there is no batter waiting to bat. The teams then change over so the fielding team goes in to bat.

No-ball

A no-ball is called when the ball:
► is bowled by the bowler without both feet in the bowling square
► is higher than the head or lower than the knee when it reaches the batter
► is aimed directly at the batter
► is wide of the non-hitting side
► hits the ground before it reaches the batter.

Other

Teams consist of six players. Each team bats for one innings. The winner is the team scoring the greatest number of rounders at the end of the match.

Rules for rounders

Equipment
- One bat.
- One ball.
- Four markers.
- A large area of flat ground with the correct pitch measurements and markings.

Aim of the game
The aim is to score more rounders than the opposing team.

Starting the game
One team bats and one team fields. The game starts with the bowler bowling to the first batsman of the opposing team. On receiving a good ball (see under No-ball), the batter must run to the first post, or may run further if possible. The remainder of the batting team continue to bat in order.

Scoring
A rounder is scored when a batter, after hitting the ball, succeeds in running around all the posts (touching the last), before the fielding team get the ball to the fourth post. Players may only score one rounder per turn. If the batter fulfils the above without hitting the ball, only half a rounder is scored.

Penalty half rounders are also awarded when:
- the bowler bowls two consecutive no-balls (see below) to the same batter
- the batter is obstructed by the fielding team
- a waiting batsman obstructs a fielder.

Batting
A batter receives one good ball and must then run to first post. If the ball goes into the backward area, the batter may not run beyond first post. The batter has the option to run on a no-ball, or receive another ball. Batters waiting on posts may only run after the ball is bowled. A runner is not obliged to run unless the player immediately behind does so. Only one batter is allowed to wait on each post at any one time. A batter may not overtake another batter.

Batters out
A batter is declared out when:
- the ball is caught from the bat or a hand touching the bat
- a fielder touches the post the batter is running to, with the ball, before the batter has touched the post
- a fielder is obstructed or the direction of the ball is deliberately altered
- a batter in front is overtaken
- the bowler has the ball in the bowling square and the batter

continues to run past the next post
- ▶ there is already a batter at the post they are running to.

The innings is over when there is no batter waiting to bat. The teams then change over so the fielding team goes in to bat.

No-ball
A no-ball is called when the ball:
- ▶ is bowled by the bowler without both feet in the bowling square
- ▶ is higher than the head or lower than the knee when it reaches the batter
- ▶ would hit the batter
- ▶ is wide of the non-hitting side
- ▶ hits the ground on the way to the batter.

Other
Teams consist of equal numbers of between six and nine players. Each team bats for two innings. The winner is the team scoring the greatest number of rounders at the end of all innings.

Session plan

Date 3.7.98
Venue Sunny School
Time 2 p.m.
Duration 45 minutes
Group Boys and girls, 8/9 years
Number in group 40

Objectives
To help students learn how to co-ordinate hitting, running, throwing and catching skills in one game.

Equipment
- ▶ One ball and four markers.

Organisation
Warm-up/introduction (5 minutes):
- ▶ three colours game (see page 24, warm-up activities for young children 1)
- ▶ copying the teacher, the teacher demonstrates two to three stretches and the class copy (see pages 24–26, stretches)
- ▶ run to a base, draw a circle with a ball, run to the next base.

Main content (30 minutes):
- ▶ running rounders (see pages 111–112, batting games)

Teaching points

Ask the students
- ▶ **How can you get to the fourth post quicker?**
  Turn quickly at the posts.
  Stay close to the markers as you turn.
- ▶ **How can you make it easier for the runners?**
  Put four extra players in the fielding team, one between each post, so the ball has an extra stop between posts; this gives the runners more time.
- ▶ **How can you make it harder for the runners?**
  Make the runners circle each post before they run on to the next.

Cool down (5 minutes):
► walk the pitch briskly, circling each post before walking on to the next post
► stretches as above; ask the group to show you.

Collect all equipment

Recap (5 minutes)

Summarise the main teaching points. Ask the students:
► How easy was it to beat the runner to fourth base?
► Does it matter in which order the fielders stand around the pitch?
► Think of two things you have learnt about catching and passing the ball.

Safety
► A tennis ball, rather than a rounders ball, can be used if the children are young and/or new to the game.
► Make sure the groups are well spaced.
► Injuries – none.

9
Athletic games

By the end of this chapter, you should be able to explain the different types of athletic events and know how to teach them. Athletic sports share many similar skills, and the activities in this chapter help students to develop and practise these skills. The chapter then lists the rules for shot put, long jump and sprinting.

Introduction

Athletics involves many varied physical activities. Unlike some other games, athletic events can be measured very objectively, for example, start and finish time, distance thrown. The skills are very technical and require consistent practice for improvements to happen. Athletics requires all the elements of fitness, although some activities will be more dependent on certain components, for example long distance running requires more stamina than short distance sprints. Athletic skills are a good foundation for all sports. They can be broken down into:

▶ **field activities** – throwing, for example shot put
▶ **field activities** – jumping, for example long jump
▶ **track activities**, for example the 100 m sprint.

Exercises for each of the above are shown in stages, leading to competition and rules for the relevant events.

The metric measurements given for the pitch and equipment are the official ones stipulated in the rules of each sport. If space and equipment are limited, you should feel free to improvise and make the best use of whatever is available.

Field activities – throwing

Throwing an implement, for example a shot, as far as possible requires a combination of strength and speed. Technique is important as the angle and speed of release largely influence distance. Balance is also important in achieving maximum power and release at the right moment.

Stage 1 *Putting action*

Objectives
To help students learn the putting technique.

Pre-game exercise
▶ Students line up and copy a standing putting action (a specific action for throwing the shot) without the ball.

Equipment
▶ One rope or net.
▶ One ball, for example a tennis ball, per pair.
▶ Two markers.

Safety
▶ Position pairs as far apart as possible.

- Do not let players collect balls that go astray unless it is safe to do so.
- Stop the whole group if balls need to be retrieved.
- Left-handed students should stand at the right end of the line.

Activity
- In pairs, students number themselves 1 and 2, stand either side of the rope. and place markers at their starting position.
- Number 1 puts the ball from standing over the rope to Number 2, who catches it and puts it back to Number 1. If students put and catch successfully, they move their markers a little further back for the next put.
- Students aim to get as far apart as possible, but must not go further than they can put.

To make the activity easier:
- encourage pairs to keep a comfortable distance apart while they are getting used to the action.

To make the activity more difficult:
- encourage pairs to move further apart and start using a heavier ball.

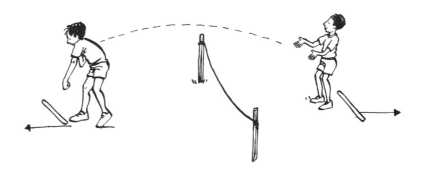

Teaching points

Ask the students
- **How do you prepare to put?**
Hold the ball next to your neck and chin, rest the ball on the middle three fingers and support it with your thumb and little finger on either side.

- **How do you release the ball?**
Keep the ball away from the palm of the hand. Stand sideways on with your weight on your back foot.
Twist your body as you transfer your weight from the back foot to the front foot.
Turn your shoulders to face forward as the arm extends in a strong forward and upward action.

Stage 2 *Foot positioning*

Objectives
To teach students how to generate power from their feet and legs prior to releasing the ball, without infringing the rules.

Equipment
▶ Two markers/lines for the start and finish lines.
▶ Markers or lines to mark out a square.

Safety
▶ Position pairs as far apart as possible.

Activity
▶ In pairs, students number themselves 1 and 2, mark the point/draw a line where the foot action starts and finishes, and mark a square (½ metre square) in front of the front marker.
▶ Number 1 practises the foot action, aiming the front foot to land in the marked square, and scores 1 point if his or her feet land in the correct sequence, 1 point if all of his or her front foot lands in the square, but loses a point if any part of either foot goes beyond the front marker.
▶ Number 2 keeps score for Number 1 and then they change roles.
▶ Students count their total number of points after 10 turns.

To make the activity easier:
▶ play the game without the marked square: score one point for the correct foot sequence and lose one point if either foot goes over the front line.

To make the activity more difficult:
▶ make foot movements quicker and more powerful; this makes it more difficult for students to stay behind the front line after the action.

Teaching points

Ask the students

▶ **How should your feet be positioned at the start of the put?**

Put your weight on your back foot, crouch down and point your foot in the opposite direction to the put.

Tuck the other leg in close behind.

▶ **How should your feet move during the put?**

Extend your front leg behind and hop into the middle of the space.

Step and transfer your weight onto your front foot. The foot should land in the marked square.

Stage 3 *Foot and putting action*

Objectives
To teach students how to co-ordinate the full putting action.

Equipment
▶ Markers/line for starting and putting point.
▶ One marker per pair.
▶ One ball per pair.

Safety
▶ Position pairs as far apart as possible.
▶ Students must try to put in a straight line.

Activity
▶ In pairs, students number themselves 1 and 2 and mark out a starting point/line and a putting line.
▶ Number 1 puts the ball as far as possible, using the full action.
▶ Number 2 catches the ball after the bounce and marks the point of Number 1's furthest put with a marker.
▶ Number 2 then rolls the ball back to Number 1, who has two more puts before students change roles. If students step over the putting line, their put cannot be marked.

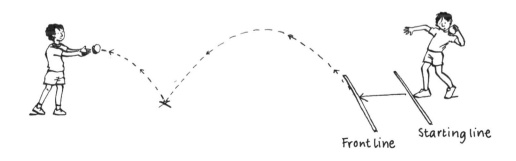

Front line   Starting line

To make the activity easier:

▶ do not be concerned with distance; do not mark where the ball lands.

To make the activity more difficult:

▶ aim for a specific but realistic target zone and count how many times the ball lands there.

Teaching points

Ask the students
▶ **What must you remember when co-ordinating the whole action?**
Concentrate on a smooth but powerful rhythm.
Transfer your weight as you release the ball; you should not just use your arm.

Stage 4 *Putting the shot*

Objectives
To help students practise the putting action using a standard weight of shot.

Equipment
▶ Markers or line for putting point.
▶ One shot per pair. Please note that if there are not enough shots, some pairs can practise with a smooth stone.

Safety
▶ Students must always wait for the teacher's call before they put the shot or move in front of the putting line to collect it.
▶ Position pairs as far apart as possible.

Activity
▶ In pairs, students number themselves 1 and 2 and mark out a putting point/line.

Volunteers and colleagues suggest that shot puts can be made from hardened mud. Alternatively, they can be made from stones that are ground down or from concrete. Different sizes are recommended for the different ages and sizes of the students, ranging from 4 kg to 7.25 kg for boys and 2.724 kg to 4 kg for girls.

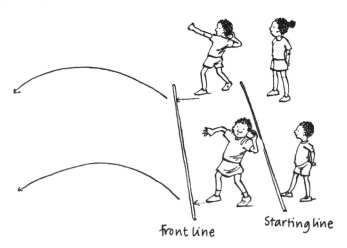

front line   Starting line

- ▶ Number 1 puts the shot from standing (without the hop) as far as possible.
- ▶ On the teacher's call, Number 1 picks up the shot, and passes it to Number 2, who, on the teacher's call, repeats the actions of Number 1.
- ▶ Students alternate puts and keep their marker positioned at the point of their furthest put.

To make the activity easier:
- ▶ use a lightweight shot.

To make the activity more difficult:
- ▶ students mark the point of their furthest put as they collect the shot. Encourage them to put further each time, providing this does not affect their technique.

Teaching points

Ask the students
- ▶ **What must you remember when putting a heavier ball or an actual shot?**
  Concentrate on your technique and do not be concerned with how far the shot travels.
  Keep the action the same as you did for Stage 1.
  Exhale as you release the ball.

Rules for shot put

Equipment
- ▶ One shot.
- ▶ An area of flat, preferably soft, ground of the correct measurements.
- ▶ One tape measure.

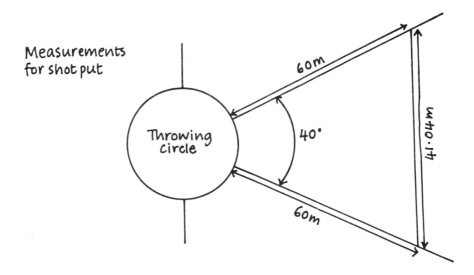

Measurements for shot put

Throwing circle

60m

40°

60m

41·0m

Aim of the event

The aim of shot put is to put the shot as far as possible. Umpires and organisers specify how many attempts (or trials) each competitor can have, which is usually between three and six.

Putting the shot

The shot is pushed rather than thrown. It is held against the neck, under the chin and must not be taken behind the shoulders. The shot rests on the middle three fingers for the whole put.

The putter begins by standing at the back of the circle, facing away from the landing sector. The putter moves from the back of the circle to the front by turning anti-clockwise and moving from the right foot to the left. This will be reversed if the putter is left-handed. As the putter faces forward, the arm should push up quickly and release the shot.

Foul puts

A foul is called when the:
► putter touches the ground outside the circle or the circle rim during the put
► putter leaves the circle before the shot has touched the ground
► shot lands outside the boundary.

A foul put in a competition is considered one trial.

Measuring a put

The distance of the put is measured from the inner edge of the circle rim to the nearest edge of the first mark made in the ground by the put. The distance is recorded to the nearest 1 cm below the distance measured.

The winner is the person with the longest distance measured for a single trial.

Other

► The putter may interrupt a trial, leave the circle, and return to begin a new trial.
► The putter must use one hand only to put the shot. It should be close to or in contact with the chin at the start of the put.
► The put must land within the marked boundaries for it to be considered a valid put.

Field activities – jumping

Jumping requires a combination of speed in the run-up, accuracy in reaching the correct take-off position and power to gain maximum height or distance. Technique is very important.

Stage 1 *The approach*

Objectives
To show students how to measure and practise their approach for long-jump.

Equipment
▶ One long line/board for take-off.
▶ One marker per student.

Safety
▶ Position pairs as far apart as possible.

Activity
▶ Students number themselves 1 and 2.
▶ Number 1 stands by an imaginary take-off line, facing backwards with the heel of his or her non take-off foot up to the line. Number 1 then runs or sprints 15 strides in the direction he or she is facing, while Number 2 places a marker where the tip of the 15th stride lands.
▶ Students change roles and then take turns to practise their approach, they run from the marker towards the take-off line. On the 15th stride, their take-off foot should land on the line; if it does not, they should move their markers forwards or backwards until their run-up becomes accurate.
▶ Students score one point if their take-off foot touches the line without any part of it landing over, no points if their take-off foot lands before the line and lose one point if any part of their take-off foot lands over the line.
▶ Students stand by the take-off line as their partners run and tell them their score after each run.

Take-off board

To make the activity easier:
▶ decrease the number of strides so the distance to run is shorter; students are then more likely to be accurate with their measurements.

To make the activity more difficult:

▶ compete in pairs, with students counting the number of times the take-off foot hits the line out of five attempts. Students must keep running at speed.

Teaching points

Ask the students
▶ **What must you remember on the approach?**
Increase your running speed to maximum. Maintain speed as you hit the line; do not be tempted to slow down to make sure your foot hits the line in the right place (adjust your markers if necessary).
Maintain a consistent stride length and rhythm throughout.

Stage 2 *The take-off*

Objectives
To encourage students to use their arms and legs efficiently on the take-off to help them gain height and distance.

Volunteers and colleagues suggest using sawdust as the landing pit or digging up existing earth to make a softer base.

Equipment
▶ One long take-off line.
▶ Soft ground or landing pit.
▶ One marker per student.

Safety
▶ Position pairs as far apart as possible.
▶ Make sure students bend their knees on landing.

Activity
▶ In pairs, students number themselves 1 and 2.
▶ Number 1 rests the take-off foot on the line and puts his or her weight on the back foot, transfers the body weight onto the front foot and jumps as far as possible.
▶ Number 2 marks the point where the first heel touches the ground.
▶ Number 1 has three attempts to jump as far as possible and then students change roles.

To make the activity easier:

▶ encourage students to concentrate on their take-off position only, and not to mark distances
▶ allow students to take one more step; this will give them more momentum which should make it easier to jump.

To make the activity more difficult:

▶ encourage students to beat their own distances each time they jump.

Teaching points

Ask the students
▶ **How should you take off from the line?**
Transfer your weight from your back foot to your front foot as you take off.
Bring your arms forward and upward in a strong movement as you jump.
Push hard into the ground with your front leg as you take off, and then extend it fully to help lift you upwards.

Stage 3 *The flight and the landing*

Objectives
To show students how to co-ordinate the take-off, flight and landing to get maximum height and distance.

Equipment
▶ Take-off line and landing pit space (pairs may need to take turns).
▶ One marker per student.
▶ One rake or equivalent to smooth the pit after each jump.

Safety
▶ Do not let students jump until the person before them is clearly out of the way and their partner has finished raking the pit.
▶ Make sure students let their partner know when they are going to jump.

Activity
▶ In pairs, students number themselves 1 and 2.
▶ Number 1 faces the pit with his or her front foot on the take-off line and body weight on the back foot. Number 1 takes off as in Stage 2, bringing the legs through, and lands as far as possible from the take-off line without any part of the body touching the pit behind during or after landing.
▶ Number 2 marks the nearest part of contact with the pit to the take-off line and then smooths the pit.
▶ Students have three turns each before changing roles.

To make the activity easier:
▶ encourage students to concentrate on their flight and landing positions only, and not mark distances
▶ allow students to take one more step; this will give them more momentum which should give them more time in the air.

To make the activity more difficult:
▶ encourage students to beat their own distances each time they jump.

Teaching points

Ask the students

▶ **What must you remember after take-off?**
Bring your back leg through, lifting your knee as high as possible.
Keep your back flat and your head straight.
Bring your take-off leg through to join the other leg as you descend.
Lift your arms above your head as you reach maximum height.

▶ **What must you remember on landing?**
Pull yourself forward by throwing your arms forward as you descend.
Land with your feet as far forward as possible but not so far forward that this makes you sit back into the pit.
Throw yourself forward as you land and do not let any part of your body touch the pit behind you.

Stage 4 *Short run and jump*

Objectives

To show students how to co-ordinate the approach, take-off, flight and landing.

Equipment

▶ Take-off line and landing pit space (pairs may need to take turns).
▶ One marker per student.
▶ One rake or equivalent to smooth the pit after each jump.

Safety

▶ Do not let students start their approach until the person before them is clearly out of the way and their partner has finished raking the pit.
▶ Make sure students let their partner know when they are going to jump.

Activity

▶ In pairs, students number themselves 1 and 2 and roughly mark out five strides from the take-off line.
▶ Number 1 runs from the mark and jumps as far as possible into the pit, putting together all the actions from Stages 1–3.
▶ Number 2 marks the nearest part of contact with the pit to the take-off line and then smooths the pit.
▶ Students have three turns each before changing roles.

To make the activity easier:
▶ concentrate on technique only, and do not mark distances.

To make the activity more difficult:
▶ encourage students to beat their own distances each time they jump and to compare distances with their partner.

Teaching points

Ask the students
▶ **What must you remember when putting the whole action together?**
Concentrate on two to three points only at a time, for example speed on the approach, height on jump, move forward out of pit.

Rules for long jump

Equipment
▶ Flat ground for a runway (approximately 30 m).
▶ A landing pit, preferably of sand or loose ground to help measurements.
▶ Ideally you should use a wooden board for take-off but a marked line can be used.
▶ One tape measure to record distances.
▶ One rake to smooth the pit after each jump.

Measurements for long jump

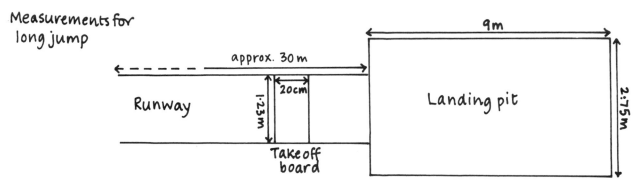

Aim of the event
The aim of the long jump is to land as far from the take-off line as possible in a single jump. When competing against other competitors, the aim is to jump the furthest.

The jump
▶ In the approach, jumpers should run as fast as possible down the runway, reaching top speed as they take off. They should take off from, on or behind, but not over, the take-off board or marked line.
▶ When taking off, jumpers should throw their legs forward and upward. The arms should go over the head and reach forward.

Foul jumps
A foul is called when a jumper:
▶ touches the ground beyond the take-off line when taking off
▶ takes off from outside the edges of the take-off board or line
▶ after jumping, walks back through the landing area.

A foul jump in a competition is considered one trial.

Measuring a jump

The jump distance is measured at a right angle to the take-off line from the nearest break in the ground made by the jumper to the take-off line. The distance is recorded to the nearest 1 cm below the distance measured.

The winner is the person with the longest distance measured for a single trial.

Track activities

Track activities involve running and this can be combined with jumping for some events, for example hurdles. Sprint running requires speed combined with strength (power) in order to cover a short distance very quickly. Long distance running requires more stamina.

Stage 1 *Starting*

Objectives
To encourage students to react and move quickly to the starting cue.

Equipment
▶ One starting line.

Safety
▶ Make sure groups are as far apart as possible.

Activity
▶ In threes, students number themselves 1 to 3.
▶ Numbers 1 and 2 line up at the start line, while Number 3 stands at the edge of the start line.
▶ As Number 3 says 'on your marks', Numbers 1 and 2 take their starting position behind the line; as Number 3 says 'set', 1 and 2 refine their position and keep still; as Number 3 says 'go', 1 and 2 sprint approximately three strides as fast as possible.

Start position

Set position

Volunteers and colleagues suggest that students, particularly girls, enjoy relay games. These may be in the form of straight running races as a final activity or as part of the warm-up. An example of relay games for the warm-up is to divide students into four equal teams, with one ball per team. Students must pass the ball over the heads and under the legs alternately until the ball reaches the last person in the line.

- Number 3 gives one point to the person who is first to leave the line, no points if there is a draw, and deducts one point if someone clearly leaves the line before 'go'.
- Numbers 1 and 2 have five chances to score points before changing roles, then Numbers 3 and 1 have a go while Number 2 keeps score, and then Numbers 3 and 2 have a go while Number 1 keeps score.
- The winner has the most points after everyone has raced each other.

Teaching points

Ask the students
- **How can you make a good start?**
  Anticipate the 'go' command.
  React and move immediately on 'go'.

Stage 2 *Starting and increasing speed*

Objectives
To encourage students to react and move quickly to the starting cue and to increase speed as quickly as possible.

Equipment
- One starting line.
- One 10 m line.

Safety
- Keep students well spaced.
- Ensure those who are not running do not obstruct the runners.

Activity
- In pairs, students number themselves 1 and 2.
- All the number 1s line up at the start line, while the Number 2s go to the 10 m mark.
- On the teacher's command of 'on your marks, set, go', Number 1s race to the line as fast as possible, while Number 2s try to judge the position of their partner (for example second, fifth).
- Number 2s then change roles with Number 1s and they keep alternating roles, trying to beat their position each time they race.

Teaching points

Ask the students

▶ **How do you increase speed quickly?**
Anticipate the 'go' command.
React and move immediately on 'go'.
Push off strongly with your legs, bring your knees forward and upward quickly, and use your arms.
Concentrate on covering as much ground as possible.

Stage 3 *Maintaining speed*

Objectives

To encourage students to maintain their maximum speed until the end of the race.

Equipment

▶ One starting line.
▶ One 100 m line.
▶ A stopwatch, digital or second hand watch if possible.

Safety

▶ Keep groups well spaced.

Activity

▶ In threes, students number themselves 1, 2 and 3.
▶ Number 1s and 3s go to the start line, and Number 2s to the 100 m line.
▶ Number 1s run to the 100 m line and tag Number 2s.
▶ Number 2s then run back to the start line and tag Number 3s.
▶ Number 3s then run to the 100 m line and tag Number 1s and so on.

To make the activity easier:
▶ decrease the distance, for example 50 m, 80 m, until students improve.

To make the activity more difficult:
▶ make the exercise competitive, for example all the Number 1s race, then the Number 2s
▶ students time themselves or each other.

Teaching points

Ask the students

▶ **How can you maintain speed over 100 m?**
Use your arms.
Relax the muscles in your face, neck, shoulders and hands.

Concentrate on lifting your knees high and extending your back leg fully before bringing it forward.
Maintain an even stride length and rhythm.

Stage 4 *Running drills*

Objectives

To encourage students to improve their running technique and increase their power for sprinting.

Equipment

▶ One starting line and one 30 m line.

Safety

▶ Make sure students are well spaced.

Activity

▶ In pairs, students number themselves 1 and 2.
▶ Number 1s walk to the line, lifting their knees high.
▶ Number 2s follow on the teacher's command.
▶ Number 1s repeat the drill back to the start line, but this time they skip, still lifting their knees high.
▶ Number 2s follow on the teacher's command.

To make the activity easier:
▶ do the exercise without rising onto the toes, concentrating on the arms and the knee lift only.

To make the activity more difficult:
▶ jump as high as possible on each lift but maintain posture and control.

Teaching points

Ask the students
▶ **How can you improve your running technique?**
Lift your knees high as you bring your back legs forward.

Extend your supporting leg fully as you rise onto your toes.
Keep your body upright.
Use your arms.

Rules for 100 m sprint

Equipment

▶ Preferably a pair of running shoes.
▶ A level surface with a start and finish line marked 100 m apart.

Aim of the event

The aim of the 100 m sprint is to reach the finish line as quickly as possible. When racing against other competitors, the aim is to finish the race first.

Starting the race

At the start of the race all competitors must be behind, but not touching, the start line. The starter will give the following commands:

- **'On your marks'** the competitors line up behind the start line
- **'Set'** the competitors get in the set position, where they are motionless on their mark
- **'Go'** on hearing the go signal, the competitors start running.

False start
A false start is where the race must be restarted, with the competitors re-lining at the start. A false start is called when:
- on the command 'set', a competitor fails to get into the set position immediately
- a competitor starts to run after the 'set' command but before the 'go' command.

A competitor making a false start is warned. A competitor making two false starts is disqualified.

The race
Competitors run in lanes for the entire race. A competitor who runs out of their lane may be disqualified.

The finish
The winner is the first person to reach the finish line with any part of their body. If there is a tie for first place, the referee may decide whether the race be run again or the result stand. Ties for the other positions may remain.

Session plan

Date 3.7.98
Venue Sunny School
Time 2 p.m.
Duration 45 minutes
Group Boys and girls, 8/9 years
Number in group 40

Objectives
To encourage students to react and move quickly to the starting cue.

Equipment
- One starting line, markers.

Organisation
Warm-up/introduction (5 minutes):
- tag – whoever gets caught becomes the new chaser.
- copying the teacher, the teacher demonstrates two to three stretches and the class copy (see pages 24–26, stretches).

Main content (30 minutes):
- 10 minutes – skipping exercises (see pages 39–40)
- 10 minutes – starting to sprint (see pages 145–146)
- 10 minutes – shuttle race (see pages 36–37, running and jumping skills).

Teaching points

Ask the students
- **How can you turn quicker?**
  Pick up or put down the marker as you turn.
  Bend your knees as you pick up/put down.

- **How can you make a good start?**
  Anticipate the 'go' command.
  React and move immediately on 'go'.

To make the activity easier:
► make sure the intervals between the commands are even.

To make the activity more difficult:
► vary the interval between commands.

Cool down (5 minutes):
► walk around running track
► draw circles activity (see warm-up).

Recap (5 minutes)

Summarise the main teaching points. Ask the students:
► How many times did you leave the mark before the 'go' command?
► Think of another way to make sure you do not leave the mark too early.

Safety
► Make sure the groups are as far apart as possible.
► Injuries – none.

10 Organising sports events

By the end of this chapter you should know how to run simple sports events and competitions.

Introduction

Sport can be enjoyed without the need to keep score or have a champion. However, students are competitive by nature. If you offer them the challenges of competition, you can help them to further their sporting and personal development. Competition presents them with pressures such as keeping control during poor performance, sustaining motivation and coping with controversial decisions. These skills can not only be improved and used in sport, but also transferred and used in many other situations, such as getting on with others and joining in school activities.

Some students will respond more positively than others to competitive situations, for example some will fear losing more than others, and you should encourage them accordingly. This chapter will give you ideas of how to organise different types of competition and other factors you need to consider, such as preparation and officiating. If running competitions is new to you, you may wish to start with a small tournament/event for a group of students you teach. Whether you choose to run competitions or whether you are asked to do so, this chapter will help you to run them efficiently and effectively.

Preparation

Any event needs preparation and its success largely depends on the effort put in beforehand. There are many factors you need to consider when organising sports games and the type you choose will depend on these. For example, you might have:
► large or small numbers
► beginners, improvers or a mix of abilities
► recreational or more serious competitors
► a range of ages
► individuals or teams
► limited access to facilities or equipment
► limited help.

There are other questions you should ask yourself before taking on the responsibility of organising a competition. For example:
► What is the minimum and maximum number of competitions for each student?
► Where can you hold the competition — is there enough space?
► Can everyone get to the venue?
► What equipment do you need?
► How important is it for teams/individuals to be evenly matched?
► Do you need helpers – if so, who will help you?
► What will be the rules for the competitions?
► How will you arrange the matches?

Whether you are organising an event within the school or an open tournament, you need to confirm your access to sites, equipment and helpers/officials. If you are recruiting helpers, make sure you explain exactly what they will need to do. Only then will you be able to judge if they are willing and able to help. At this stage, you can decide what sort of competition is appropriate and start to plan. Plans will vary according to the type of event you are organising. You will need to devise a results sheet to keep a record of scores.

Type of event

Competitions may range from a simple friendly match between two teams within your group, to a multi-sports all-day competition for different age groups. The nature of the different types of events you can organise is explained in this section and this will help you to decide which is the most appropriate.

Knock-out competitions

Many competitions are of a knock-out form. The disadvantage of this format is that after one match 50 per cent of teams or players are out of the tournament. If you do run a competition of this nature, you might consider running a second knock-out competition for first round losers. This ensures every team/player has at least two matches.

You should structure the draw so the strongest teams/players do not play each other in the first round. This is called seeding. For example, the following teams are seeded 1—4 respectively: Yellows, Greys, Blues and Greens. The other teams/players can then be drawn out of a hat to decide who they should play. In cases where numbers are uneven (those that are not 4, 8, 16, 32, and so on), you may have to give certain teams/players a bye, which means they go through to the next round without having to play. It is best to spread the byes evenly throughout the draw and give them in rank order to the seeded players. So the Yellows would

First round/ Quarter-final	Semi-final	Final	Winner
Yellows (1)	Yellows		
Bye		Yellows	
Greens (4)	Reds		
Reds			Yellows
Oranges	Blues		
Blues (3)		Greys	
Purples	Greys		
Greys (2)			

have a bye into the second round. The order of the matches is referred to as the order of play, and is done according to the availability of players/teams, umpires, pitches and equipment.

Step-by-step organisation

1 Count the number of teams/players.

2 Decide how many teams/players to seed.

3 Rank the seeds and place them in the draw.

4 Place byes in draw.

5 Draw the remaining teams/players and position them in the draw.

6 Draw up order of play.

7 Decide if you are running a competition for first round losers: If yes, go back to Step 1, if no, proceed to Step 8.

8 Organise the matches (see pages 154 and 155 for checklists).

Round-robin competitions

Round-robin competitions are very popular in sport because everyone can play an equal number of matches and no one is out in the first round. There can be a number of teams/players in a group, all of whom play each other. If there are many entries or you want to find an eventual winner of the event, you can put people into a number of groups and then run a knock-out event for the winners of each group (and if time allows for those who finish second and third in their group). Alternatively, if there are two groups, the top two scorers in each group could go through to a semi-final; the winner of Group 1 plays the runner-up of Group 2, while the winner of Group 2 plays the runner-up of Group 1. The winners will then go through to the final, where they will compete for first and second place.

It is advisable if there is more than one group to seed the better teams/players so they are spread evenly among the groups (unless you are running an A and B event; the A for the better players and the B for the weaker ones). In the following example, the seeded teams are:

1 Team A Group 1

2 Team A Group 2

3 Team B Group 2

4 Team B Group 1.

This helps to balance the groups in terms of standard and prevent a situation where good teams or players do not go through to further stages because all the best players are in their group. The following example shows how you might organise a round robin event for eight players or teams. You can set up a results card to fill in the scores.

Group 1

	A	B	C	D
A				
B				
C				
D				

Group 2

	A	B	C	D
A				
B				
C				
D				

The order of play is:

▶ Group 1
A v C	B v D
A v D	B v C
A v B	C v D

▶ Group 2
A v C	B v D
A v D	B v C
A v B	C v D

The knock-out stages are:

Semi-final	Final	Winner
Winner Group A		
Runner up Group B		
Winner Group B		
Runner up Group A		

Step-by-step organisation

1 Count the numbers of teams/players.

2 Decide how many groups.

3 Decide how many teams/players to seed.

4 Rank seeds in the group (for example, Seed 1 in Group 1, Seed 2 in Group 2).

5 Draw the remaining teams/players to decide which group they are in, for example Group 1C.

6 Draw up the order of play.

7 Decide if there are further knock-out stages, for example winners of groups playing off.

8 Draw up the order of play for further stages.

9 Organise matches (see page 155 for checklists).

10 Draw up a checklist for equipment and make sure you have access to everything you will need.

11 Make sure you have access to first aid.

12 Distribute up-to-date rules of the competition to all the competitors or participating schools.

Leagues and fixtures

If you want to arrange competitions with other teams in your area, for example one school versus another, you may wish to organise a league where teams play against each other over a period of time. The format may be knock-out or round-robin. Alternatively you may arrange some friendly fixtures, which are one-off competitions on a certain day. You can run these according to age or ability, for example, U 12 and U 16 leagues/fixtures. If you are organising a league, it may be best to set up a small committee of people to help you, for example, a representative from the other teams. Whichever format you decide will need organisation.

Step-by-step organisation

1 Find an organiser or contact in the other team/s.

2 Clarify dates, times, venues, equipment, officials.

3 Clarify numbers, ages, standards and organise the event accordingly, for example 5 versus 5 U 15 football.

4 Make sure both teams know the rules and regulations, including what to do if teams fail to show or are late.

5 Ensure results are recorded.

6 Check everything will run smoothly on the day (see below for checklist).

On the day

Most of the organisation for matches or competition can be done prior to the event. However, certain things need to be checked on the day. The following checklist shows you the sort of things you need to consider to help the event run smoothly.

On the day of the competition, you should ensure:
► all the equipment is ready and in working order
► you have access to first aid support
► you display a timetable of matches so students and umpires/officials know when they are needed
► a captain is appointed for each team
► captains/helpers hand in results immediately
► results are displayed so everyone can follow the progress of the competition
► you treat all teams/competitors fairly, for example giving teams equal rest times, equal numbers of matches
► teams can be identified, for example by colour of kit, shirts on/off
► you arrive in plenty of time to check the facilities are prepared and safe
► students are met and told where to go
► helpers know what to do and where to go
► students know where they can get some water
► any spectators are out of danger
► people know where to go if they need help
► there are procedures in case of bad weather or teams failing to turn up
► encourage the students to play fairly and to enjoy the taking part. As Baron Pierre de Coubertin, founder of the modern Olympic Games, stated:
'The important thing in sport is not to win but to take part; just

as the important thing in life is not the triumph but the struggle. The essential thing is not to have conquered but to have fought well.'

Officiating

If you are taking on the role of an official, your aim is to ensure students play safely, fairly and compete within the rules of the game (see Chapter 4). This will help them to have positive experiences of competition. You need to keep control of situations, and be decisive and firm with your actions at all times. You are responsible for recording the result and telling competitors the final score. In addition, check you have everything you need before you start, for example whistle, equipment, the teams, the rules, pencil and paper. The following general guidelines will help you if you have to umpire matches.

Tips for umpiring

- ▶ Try to have use of a whistle – you will need this to start the games, and to stop play for fouls or other reasons.
- ▶ Call all decisions loudly, clearly and with confidence.
- ▶ As a general rule, you should go through the following stages when you interrupt play: blow the whistle; call the infringement,

---

RECOMMENDATIONS FROM VSO VOLUNTEERS AND THEIR NATIONAL COLLEAGUES

FOR PREPARING AND RUNNING A SPORTS COMPETITION
- ▶ Plan well in advance – draw up a list of what needs to be done, what equipment is needed and delegate responsibility.
- ▶ Be prepared for last minute organisation on the day – sometimes it is very hard to predict who will arrive on the day and therefore you need to adapt and plan quickly according to the situation.
- ▶ Meet regularly to check on progress and set deadlines for tasks.
- ▶ Make sure the media are given advanced warning of the event.

- ▶ Take photographs of the event to promote it in the future.
- ▶ Choose a venue that will be easily accessible.
- ▶ Ensure that the date, venue and time are clearly publicised.
- ▶ Be prepared to improvise at the last minute.
- ▶ Inform the school well in advance to allow time for organisation and to enable students to practise for events.
- ▶ Award prizes at the end to motivate students and to show appreciation.
- ▶ Award points for participation or completing a race to discourage students from giving up.

- ▶ Try to organise team kit for your students – identity is very important to them and will motivate them to perform well and enjoy themselves. You could ask local businesses to sponsor your team by providing T-shirts for the students.
- ▶ Inter-school sports days can be very motivating for students – they need to be organised well in advance, for example 6–7 weeks, and preparation includes organising transport, teams, practices and prizes, for example sweets and drinks. You should visit the school you are competing with nearer the time to check they are prepared for the event.

for example 'obstruction'; call the penalty and the team/player to whom it is awarded, for example 'free pass to the reds'.

▶ Never change your decisions – if you remain firm with them, even if you fear they may be wrong, players will respect you and not be tempted to persuade you to change your mind.

After the event

It is important for students to walk away from competitions feeling positive. Whether they win or lose, play well or badly, they should be encouraged to:

▶ congratulate or thank the opposing team/player for the match
▶ congratulate or support team mates
▶ thank the official
▶ think about what they have learned from the match and what can be improved
▶ watch the remaining matches that are in action
▶ help clear away any equipment
▶ stay for a presentation or announcement of results
▶ feel pleased with themselves if they tried hard
▶ tell you or someone in charge they are leaving, so you know they have not just disappeared
▶ change out of wet clothing
▶ drink plenty of fluids and have some food to replace lost energy.

After the event you are responsible for ensuring any equipment or rubbish is cleared away, collecting results and making sure no one is left behind. While events are fresh in your mind, write down what went well and what you could do to organise things better next time. Remember to refer to these notes before you organise your next event.

Recap/summary

There are many factors to consider when you organise sports events and competitions. Good preparation helps the event to run smoothly on the day. You should consider which format is most suitable for the students before you start to organise. Write down comments as soon as possible after the event to help you with your organisation of events in the future.

Glossary

Bye A situation where a player or team who has not drawn an opponent (for example if there is an odd number of competitors) goes directly through to the next round of a knock-out competition without having to play.

Court The boundaries of an area in which play is allowed, for example in volleyball.

Defensive In invasive games, for example hockey and basketball, the defensive team/player is the one attempting to gain possession of the ball.

Dig A technique in volleyball in which the ball is played from outstretched forearms, usually when the ball is travelling very fast or very low.

Draw A method of determining the first round of matches in a knock-out competition.

Dribble In hockey – keeping the ball close to the stick while moving. In football – keeping the ball close to the feet while moving. In basketball and handball – bouncing the ball while moving.

Fielding In cricket, rounders and softball – bowling the ball to the batting team and retrieving the ball when it is hit, in an attempt to get the batting team out.

Goalkeeper A player responsible for guarding the goal and preventing goals from being scored.

Grid A designated area, within which players must stay, to ensure safety.

Innings In cricket – when the batting team is out or when a certain number of overs have been bowled.

Intercept To gain possession of the ball as one player attempts to pass to another player on the same team.

Jump ball Starts a game of basketball where the referee throws the ball above the heads of two opposing players, who attempt to tap it to their team mates.

Knock-out A type of competition in which the losing teams/players are out and the winning teams/players go through to the next round, until there is one eventual winner.

Lay-up Taking two steps towards the goal and jumping up on one leg as the player attempts to shoot.

Leagues/fixtures A round-robin tournament played over a period of time. Each arranged match between two teams/players is called a fixture.

Mark To stay close to an opposing player in an attempt to stop him or her receiving the ball.

Net In volleyball – it divides the court in half and separates one team from another. Teams must play the ball over the net. In netball and basketball – it can be used as part of the goal, where it is attached to the ring. In football, hockey and handball – it can be used to drape around the goal posts to stop the ball as a goal is scored and make it easier to see if a goal is scored by trapping the ball.

Offensive In invasive games, the offensive team/player is the one in possession of the ball.

Offside In hockey – the offside rule is no longer enforced. In netball – players are offside if they go outside their permitted areas, although players may lean or touch the ball outside their permitted areas provided their body does not touch the ground. In football – when the ball is played forward by the attacking team in the opposition's half, attacking players are offside if they are in front of the last but one opposing player. In rugby – when attacking, players are offside and can take no part in the game if they are in front of the player in possession of the ball or the player who has last played the ball. If defending a scrummage and breakdowns of play, players are offside if they are in front of an imaginary line which runs immediately behind the scrum and parallel to the goal line. When defending line-outs, defensive players not in the line-out are offside if they are not 10 m from an imaginary line running through the line-out and parallel to the goal line.

Order of play The order of the matches played in a competition.

Over In cricket – six balls bowled from one wicket to another.

Push In hockey – to pass the ball with the stick remaining in contact with the ball for as long as possible during the action. In football – to pass the ball with the foot remaining in contact with the ball for as long as possible during the action.

Put A specific action for throwing the shot.

Rally In volleyball – the number of consecutive times the ball goes over the net and into court.

Round-robin A form of competition in which the teams/players are divided into groups and each team/player plays all of the other teams/players in the group.

Seeding A ranking order for competitions used to place the better players/teams in different parts of the draw with the intention of them playing each other in the later stages.

Sport A competitive game or physical event. Although school teachers primarily relate to the term physical education, the term sport as used in this handbook can refer to both physical education and sport.

Strike A general term meaning to hit the ball. In volleyball – an attempt to hit the ball down over the net. In softball and teeball – an attempt to hit the ball with the bat.

Students In this book, the term students refers to children and young people from primary to secondary school level who are being encouraged by teachers or other helpers to take part in sport.

Tackle In football – to use the feet to steal possession of the ball from an opposing player. In hockey – to use the stick to steal possession of the ball from an opposing player. In basketball and handball – to use the hands to steal possession of the ball from an opposing player. In rugby – to use the hands to bring down an opposing player in possession of the ball or touch an opposing player in touch rugby.

Tag Touching a player you are chasing to indicate he or she has been caught.

Teachers In this book, the term teachers may refer to school teachers and anyone involved with teaching sport and physical education, for example youth and community workers and refugee camp workers.

Tee An object on which to rest the ball, to make it easier to strike.

Volley In volleyball – to pass the ball using the fingers of both hands in such a way that the ball does not come to rest on the hands and the ball is propelled upwards and forwards.

Wicket In cricket – the three stumps at either end of the pitch that the batter attempts to defend from the fielding team.

Wrong-foot (verb) Pretending to move or throw in one direction, so the opposition moves to cover this, leaving a space to move or throw to the other side.

Index